Stretching The Scope Of Sacred Service

Magnifying The Mission And Multiplying The Ministry Of The Church

Everette W. Frye, Sr., D.Min.

Frye POWER Publishing Concern

Edited by Della R. Coles,
Co-entrepreneur of Coldin Creations
Front Cover design by M. Juanita Riggins

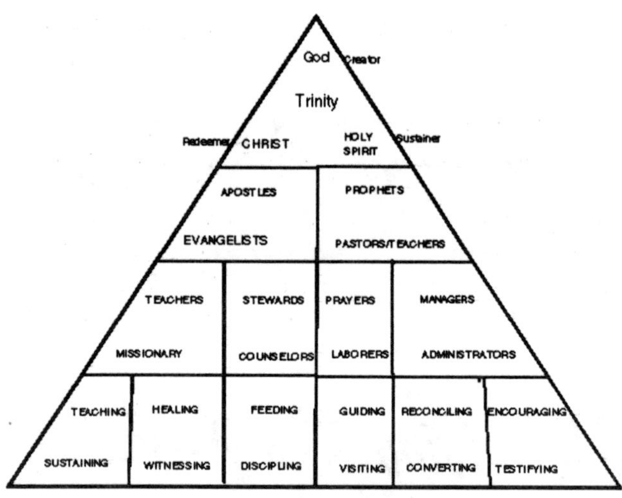

P.O.W.E.R. TO GOD'S PEOPLE

ISBN: 0-9662787-0-4
Library of Congress Card Catalog Number: 98-92384
First Printing - Fall 1997
Scripture quotations from The King James Version of the Bible
Copyright©1997 by Everette W. Frye, Sr.
All rights reserved. No part of this publication may be reproduced in any form without the prior permission of the copyright owner.
Published by Frye P.O.W.E.R. Publishing Concern
Post Office Box 750
Lynn, MA 01903-0950

Printed in the United States of America
By Morris Publishing
3212 E. Highway 30
Kearney, NE 68847
1-800-650-7888
Fax: 308-237-0263

ACKNOWLEDGMENTS

I am grateful and thankful to the Almighty God for granting me the opportunity to minister in His name and the desire to begin and complete this my first book, after having had a desire to write a book for nearly thirty years.

I am indebted to a very large number of persons living and deceased who in numerous ways made the writing of this book possible.

I owe more than words can express to my wife, Vivian; my mother, Edmonia Brooks; our children, Acquetta and Everette; my sister and brother, Edna and Willie; and other family members, friends and colleagues for their ongoing support and encouragement when for me writing a book was only a far off dream.

Acknowledgments are given and appreciation is extended to the members of my present church, Saint Luke Christian A.M.E. Zion; to the members of my previous pastorates, especially to the Reverend Dr. Curtis M. Cofield, who licensed and ordained me to the Christian Ministry and insisted that I pursue higher education to be fully equipped for my task; to my Presiding Elder, Rev. Nathaniel Perry; and my Presiding Prelate, Bishop George W. C. Walker, Sr.; because it was through those experiences that I developed a practical understanding of the mission and ministry of the Church and began to turn my dream into a book.

Thanks to Steve Viglione, author, publisher and owner of Lighthouse Publications, who provided advice and consultation in self-publishing; to John Anderson, Director of Printing Services at Gordon College, and Regina Shearer, Director of Enrollment Management at Gordon College, for technical assistance; to Thelma Sullivan, publisher of the Black Pages of New England for helping me to keep my dream alive; to Lura Smith, Assistant to The President at Middlesex Community College; and to Louis and Grace Sibley for constant friendly advice.

A very special word of thanks to Della Coles, Church Secretary and co-entrepreneur of Coldin Creations (a desk-top publishing enterprise - Everett, MA), who read and edited the manuscript, who kept me motivated to complete my writing, and offered invaluable suggestions about grammar and style; and much appreciation to M. Juanita Riggins, who took my ideas and put them into a sketch for the cover design of this book. All of these persons, and many, many more are the true authors and finishers of this book.

Table of Contents

INTRODUCTION

"Enlarge the places of thy tent, and let them stretch forth the curtains of thine habitations: spare not, lengthen thy cords, and strengthen thy stakes; for thou shalt break forth on the right hand and on the left." Isaiah 54:2-3a

The cry of the prophet Isaiah to a people caught in the social and spiritual malaise of their day must be the same urgent cry of the modern day prophet to the individual Christian and to the Christian Church of the twentieth and twenty-first century. Our call, commission and challenge is to continually stretch the scope of our service both in the church and in the community. We are called to have an active faith in God, even in the worst of times, and to have the confidence in His word that He will magnify our mission and multiply our ministry.

This is a book that struggles with the unfolding mysteries of what it means to be a "minister" of God and to be on a "mission" for God. It is also a sharing of a personal journey and struggle to find meaning and purpose both in life in general and in the Christian Church in particular. I spent the first forty years of my life, like those in the Bible (i.e., Moses, the impotent man at the Pool of Bethesda, etc.) struggling with the meaning and purpose of my life. It was after many years of ambiguity and ambivalence that I became aware that God had a plan for my life. I hope that through the reading and reflecting of the thoughts within this book, there might be those who have a deeper understanding of their purpose and destiny in life.

This book is written simply for those who simply want to read and get a simple understanding of what is written. Because of the simplistic style used in this book it is not necessary to read with a dictionary, lexicon or commentary in hand. In fact, even the scriptures are written out rather than just inserting the Bible book, chapter and verse leaving it up to the reader to find the scripture. In this way the book can be read through quickly and applied immediately. The King James Version is used throughout the book. (That is only because the author is more familiar with the K.J.V.). The book is structured in such a way that it can be easily remembered. Through the use of alliteration, where each chapter and phase of the book begins with the letter "D", the chapters can be remembered. Because of the progression from departure to destination, the process and unfolding of the mission of the ministry becomes apparent. This book might serve as a means and method, a way to diagnose where the congregation is in its overall mission and ministry. It then allows for development as a resource book for stretching the scope of the mission and ministries within the local church. The move of God in Christ began when God sent His Son into the world. The move of God continues as He sends workers into the vineyard to perform needed service to His glory and honor.

We are called to be missionaries and the Church is called to be missionary in its outreach. As individuals we are called to be servants and our task is to serve our age according to the will and by the power of God. In Stretching The Scope of Sacred Service, the book begins with those "Wise Men" of Matthew's account of the birth narrative of Jesus. The first seekers, who in all probability, became missionaries and ministers back in their own country and in their own hometowns. The book concludes with our final destination at the end of the Kingdom Age.

Each of us must at some point in life choose to follow Christ and become His disciples. When we accept being accepted by Him, He will send us forth as His workers. Chapter I tells us of this Departure into the ministry. Chapter II Tells us of the Demands of the ministry. Our mission places demands on us and our ministry is demanding in its scope and its expectations. When Christ tells us *"Follow Me"* He leads us into a calling based upon who we are and what the needs are in our field of ministry. There is much work to be done for others and because Christ has wrought a work in us, we are obliged to become partners with Him as He seeks to work through us into the lives of others.

In Chapter III we are reminded that we should perform our ministry not only because we are commanded to do it, but there should also be a love and desire within us to go where Christ tells us to go and to do what He tells us. We are compelled by our love for others and we are propelled by the love of the Spirit of Christ. We love God and we love others because God first loved us.

There is a continued need to understand where God is at work and in whom and through whom God is working. We must always ask the question of the Disciples, "Lord, is it I?" and be willing to respond, "Here am I, send me." Chapter IV explains how we Discover the will of God in the individual Christian and in the Church, while Chapter V, Discernment, spells out ways whereby we might be able to further discern the will of God. Once the ministry within the local church has been discovered and discerned, there must be a structure and organization within the specific ministry and between the ministries within the body of the church. Chapter VI gets into the Design of Ministry. Chapter VII looks at the Development and deployment of the ministry. The work of the church does not get done or done effectively unless it is first developed and then deployed where it is needed. Chapters VIII and IX spell out the many Distinctions and Diversities of ministry. Many churches fail to be all that they can be because either there is too much overlap where different people are doing the same task, while calling themselves by different titles, or there are too few positions in the body of the church to cover the multi-faceted work of the church and to fulfill its vast ministry.

In **Deuteronomy 2:3** God told Moses to tell Israel *"Ye have compassed this mountain long enough: turn you northward."* Chapter X tells us that we have not only a mission and a ministry, but we also have a Destination. Many churches have become stuck doing the same thing over and over again. Rather than having fifty years of ministry they have had one year of ministry duplicated fifty times. This book is an effort to get us from continuing to play **"Let's go around the mountain."** Chapter X tells us that we have an ultimate destination. God's Bible has a progression which begins at the beginning of God's plan and program for humanity and the Bible concludes with the completed program of God. This process only happens when there are those who are willing to be servants of God and are willing to be sent where He desires them to go and to do and be what He desires.

May God bless you in your mission and ministry and may you find fulfillment in all that you do and finally hear Him say **"Well Done."**

Everette W. Frye, Sr. D.Min.
Summer 1997

CHAPTER 1

THE DEPARTURE INTO THE MINISTRY

In Matthew's Gospel **(Matthew 2:1-12)** we are told a story about "wise men" who had an encounter with Jesus, who was "born King of the Jews." The climax, but not the end of the story, tells us that when they had found "The King of the Jews" they "departed" into their own country "another way."

This book is an attempt to prompt the "wise" men and women of our churches to "depart another way." As we progress rapidly toward the beginning of another century and another millennium, we must continually review how we have being doing ministry. We must be wise enough to consider the possibility of doing ministry "**another way.**" Jesus told His disciples, those whom He "Sent to Serve," that they were to be "wise as serpents" **(Matthew 10:16)**.

To "**depart**" on the one hand means to leave or to quit doing something. On the other hand, "**depart**" means to vary or deviate from a regular course or customary way of doing something. Departure in the mission of the ministry is starting on a new course of action that will lead to an expanded and exciting way of service. The wise men did not change their destination but they diverged from the customary way of proceeding to their goal.

When Jesus sent out the Twelve Apostles and the Seventy He gave them instructions that expanded their mission and their ministry in new and radical ways. Often the defining of our mission and our ministry are by what has been historically and traditionally done by the church. These ways of defining mission/ministry are used rather than thinking of new creative ideas and being open to new revelations. When God's People departed from captivity in Babylon, their pilgrimage to the Land of Promise was to be a new era. In **Isaiah 43:18-19,** God tells the returning captives, *"Remember ye not the former things, neither consider the things of old. Behold, I will do a new thing; now it shall spring forth; shall ye not know it? I will even make a way in the wilderness, and rivers in the desert."* That is an exciting promise of God's plan to stretch the scope of our service. It also magnifies possibilities of ministry in and through the People of God, which is the Church.

Our problem today is that too often we continue in the old ruts on our path toward our goal rather than seeking to find where God is making a new "way in the wilderness." Paul tells us that there are many ministries although there is one ultimate mission. In **I Corinthians 12:4-6** Paul says: *"Now there are diversities of gifts, but the same Spirit. And there are differences of administrations, but the same Lord. And there are diversities of operations, but it is the same God which worketh all in all."*

This tells us that the Church must have a variety of gifts and services. The Church must also have a variety of methods for using the gifts and doing the services. But, the Church must also realize that all of the ministries done in and through the Church are done by the will of God and for the glory of God.

Again God speaks through the Prophet Isaiah to tell Israel to *"Enlarge the place of thy tent, and let them stretch forth the curtains of thine habitations: spare not, lengthen thy cords, and strengthen thy stakes"* **(Isaiah 54:2-3a)**. It is God's will for us today, as for ancient Israel, to prepare us for a broad-based ministry. We must continue to hear His challenge to our present age to equip and prepare the members of the church for a variety of ministries.

We must depart from the way of thinking that the preacher/pastor is the only "minister" in the congregation. It is important that our thoughts lead us from the ancient way of thinking that God calls sheep to be shepherds, and shepherd only. We must also realize that preparation for sacred service, both in and out of the Church, is mainly a call from God to the Church and by the Church. The Scriptures are the "**road map**" and "**marching orders**" for the Body of Christ, which is the Church of God.

Christ called upon His Church to be the "avant-garde." His Church is to be out front and ahead of the times in which it finds itself. This is necessary to lead it's generation to new and higher heights. We have great institutions of "higher" learning, but God's Word tells us that the church is God's vehicle for change and that Christ has placed gifted individuals in the Church for the equipping of saints, for the fulfilling of this mission and for the varied work of ministry. In the Early Church, at the closing of the Cannon of the New Testament, the Church was continuously expanding the sphere of it's outreach. This Church was stretching the scope of its various tasks and duties within the Body. Over the years of Church history the mission has become more concerned with the maintenance of the institution than with the ministry to its community. Also, the ministry has become more confined to the clergy. Due to this shift of mission and ministry, the Church has dwindled in its effectiveness as "Salt" and "Light." The Church of today has become more self-serving. It lacks the workers needed to fulfill the Great Commission, and its goal of carrying the Gospel to the ends of the earth and to bring the Kingdom of Heaven to earth.

For the Church to fully be the Church, and for there to be a new departure in our mission and in our ministry, we must seek to follow God's leading and God's way. There are several necessary steps to this process of moving out and stretching forth in a God-directed path.

First, our ministry must become less theoretical and technological, and it must become more tactical. We must find innovative ways of doing things rather than talking about the things done. Our religion has become more reflective and less responsive. To be missionary people is to be people on the move. We are called to be *"doers of the word"* **(James 1:22)**. We often spend too much of our time in speculation and too little time in application. There are times when we can act too quickly, but our problem is, too often, we act too late. Then we often rely on our own technology, our scientific way of doing things rather than consulting God's Word to find God's way. Christ promised us a Guide who would lead us in the right way. The people of God are not only to be "Spirit fed"; we are also to be "Spirit-led."

Second, our departure into a new way of doing ministry must become more descriptive and less diagnostic. Our calling is not to take things apart and study them for the sake of study. Our call is to bring wholeness to a broken world. It does not take "rocket scientists" to tell us that our world is broken. We spend much of our time getting a firm grip on the obvious rather than ministering to what we see. When the disciples of Jesus asked Him, *"Who did sin, this man, or his parents, that he was born blind? Jesus answered, Neither hath this man sinned, nor his parents: but that the works of God should be made manifest in him"* **(John 9:2-3)**. This man had been blind from birth (forty years). There were those who were continually diagnosing his case and trying to find out the cause, rather than ministering to his need. Jesus dealt with the problem of the man's blindness rather than blaming the man, his parents or society for the man's condition. Jesus tells us as individuals and as the Church to *"Let your light so shine before men, that they may see your good works, and glorify your Father which is in heaven"* **(Matthew 5:16)**.

It is good to be able to develop the ability to analyze things and to explain all of the mysteries of life. It is a good thing to be able to write great dissertations and treatises on deep and profound subjects. The sad reality is that while brilliant minds are contemplating profound ideas, people are living in blindness and misery.

Third, the Church is to be practical, not philosophical. We all have our own opinion on most things. What makes our ministry functional is in following God's "**blueprint**" for ministry and His "**road map**" for mission. We cannot do things our way and follow our own path, but in every situation we must seek and follow the will of God. Again, too much learning can be as dangerous as too little learning. Festus told the Apostle Paul **(Acts 26:24)**, *"Paul, thou art beside thyself; much learning doth make thee mad."* God warned Adam and Eve in the Garden of Eden to eat not from the tree of knowledge of good and evil **(Genesis 2:17)**. There is a place for education and knowledge. However, there is a danger in allowing education and knowledge to cause the minister to depart in the wrong direction. The mission and ministry of the church can become bogged down in contemplation and speculation while society suffers from disintegration and degradation.

Fourth, our ministry must be more biblical than theological. Often our young men and women are studying Christianity under instructors who do not believe in Christ. All theologies are not Bible based or Bible centered, but God's written Word is suitable for correction, and for training in righteousness **(II Timothy 3:16)**. Theology is no better or worst than the theologian, whereas, God's Word says *"Let God be* *true, but every man a liar"* **(Romans 3:4)**. We need thinkers. We need philosophers and theologians. However, we can never forget the deeper need for practical, biblical ministers who are true to God's word, His will, and His way. There are dangers today because there are so many theories, theses, and teachings about religion. The only way to decide which is the right way is to seek God's way. We can know a lot about God and yet do not know God. Ultimately our departure into a broader and deeper ministry should lead us into a deeper encounter with God.

Fifth, and last, our determination for our ministry and our departure on our mission must be more scriptural than systematic. Much of God's word does not fit into our system of doing things. There is a reality of life where the whole is greater than the sum of its parts. We cannot fully comprehend God's way of causing His purpose for His world. David says in **Psalm 139:6**, *"Such knowledge is too wonderful for me; it is high, I cannot attain unto it."* Paul says in **I Corinthians 13:12** that, "For now we see through a glass darkly." We must search the scriptures and in our search we must be open to the leading and guiding of the Holy Spirit. We do not have to see the journey's end, but we must believe and trust that it is God that is leading us and that God knows the way and the end, that He knows our direction and our destination.

The Church must ever seek to maintain a healthy balance in our ministry and in our mission. While we must be philosophical, professional and public in our vocation, we must also be practical, and seek to be personal and private in our spiritual walk with God and His people. We must strive to be like the "wise men" at the beginning of this chapter who were wise as serpents and harmless as doves, who found the Saviour and departed "**another way.**"

CHAPTER 2

THE DEMANDS OF THE MINISTRY

We live in a world today filled with "needy" people. Everywhere we look, we see souls troubled and harried by the stress of personal and social situations. There are ever increasing percentages of suicides and homicides that suggest the high level of pressure and tension today.

My assumption is that things are not so drastically different today than they were when I was a child, or before I was born, or over the past centuries. We have improved in many areas of societal life, and yet seemingly there are the same basic ills in our environment today as there have been throughout recorded history.

From today's medium we see and hear of the breakdown of the quality of life as we believe that the quality of life should be. Although we have hopes and aspirations that life will become progressively better, we find that things continually remain the same or deteriorate. The sad indictment placed on today's church member is that the issues of life and death are so remote. The churches today are not involved in the big concerns of life.

We see people everyday dying, and we can, even as the priest and the Levite, pass by on the other side **(Luke 10:30-37)**. The human condition is no less a concern today than it was in the first century. Nor is it any less a concern than it was in the first and second verses of the tenth chapter in the Gospel of Luke. Jesus sent out seventy missionaries into every city and place, where He would also come. In sending out the seventy He said unto them, *"The harvest truly is great, but the labourers are few"*.

For those who are conscious and concerned about the conditions of our time, it is quite impossible to not feel and be affected by the "pull" from without, from our environment, and the social concerns and conditions that we find all around us. Constantly the factors of our environment draws us to and fro. Some of the factors that engage our thinking are the same that confronted first century Christians. The call to ministry today is no different from the call given by Christ to the first disciples. The demands placed on us today, as the twentieth century Church on the brink of the twenty-first century, and the modern

Christians in a secularized society, are given to us as a part of that same Great Commission uttered by the resurrected Christ nearly two thousand years ago.

Before we can consider ourselves Christ-like or followers of Christ, we must begin to identify and understand our "call" to service and servanthood as a "demand" placed on us by both God and our fellow humans.

THE NEED:

Throughout His ministry Christ pointed out the need for us, as His followers, to be involved in service to others. In both the Gospels **(Matthew 9:37)** and **(Luke 10:2)** Christ speaks of His concern and compassion for society. He says that *"The harvest truly is great, but the laborers are few... "* Christ expects, no, He demands and commands us to be involved in meeting the needs of the masses. It is clear that our call is to serve this present age.

This concern of Christ is the same concern raised by the Old Testament prophets. **Micah 6:8** is very clear in this demanding call to service. Micah says that God *"Hath showed thee, O man, what is good; and what doth the Lord requires of thee, but to do justly, and to love mercy, and to walk humbly with thy God?"* This prophet simply and succinctly defines the call to the world and the churches for the need of service. What the world needs is justice, mercy and love. Considering everything stated about human needs and human desires, drives and demands, our basic daily requirements remain "justice," "mercy," and "love."

Christ also begins His ministry by stating the societal demands placed on Him. **Luke 4:18-19** records these words echoed from the Old Testament prophet Isaiah **(Isaiah 61:1-4)** assessment of human needs. *"The Spirit of the Lord is upon me, because he hath anointed me to preach the gospel to the poor; he hath sent me to heal the broken-hearted, to preach deliverance to the captives, and recovering of sight to the blind, to set at liberty them that are bruised, to preach the acceptable year of the Lord."*

These demands stated by Christ in His first sermon on this Old

Testament text could be titled, "The Demands of The Ministry." This is a sermon preached to every true Christian and a service expected from every true Christian. What we proclaim in our message and what we provide in our ministry should be no less than this.

Finally James, the brother of our Lord states in his letter (**James 1:26-27**) that if there are any persons among us who claim to be religious and do not follow the dictates explained by our religion, then we are deceiving ourselves and our religion is in vain. God called us to be "doers" of God's word and not hearers only. *"Pure religion and undefiled before God and the Father are this, to visit the fatherless and widows in their affliction, and keep himself unspotted from the world."*

THE DUTY:

There was a question asked many years ago to a person trying to escape responsibility. This person was attempting to avoid giving an answer to a direct and accusatory inquisition by his Creator. The question was, *"Where is Abel thy brother?"* The answer to the question was a question that begs an answer. *"Am I my brother's keeper?"* **(Genesis 4:9)** These are both unavoidable questions, God's question to Cain and Cain's question to God. Each of us must answer both questions with our lives. As Christians, and as every person alive, we are responsible for the welfare of others. As Christians we are not only responsible to and for others, but we are also accountable to God, our Creator, for our actions and our inactions.

We must never fail to realize that we live for a purpose, therefore, we must live purposeful lives. There is a demand placed on us by the times in which we live. The sense of duty is a constant pull from without by those in need. We are drawn by the forces and factors within our environment.

There is no humane way of escaping the question of responsibility. God did create us to indeed be our brothers/sisters keepers. Our neighbor has a right to expect help from us. Today we have greatly lost the sense of "duty." We have become numb to the pull of the pain and plight of others.

The Christian life is a calling to a life of ministry, a life of "service." God called us to serve Him and humanity. The Apostle Paul understood this responsibility of service and the role and relationship of servanthood. It would take the writing of another book to point out the number of times Paul spoke of his life as one of ministry. He followed in the life style of Christ in serving his present age. **Matthew 20:28** and **Mark 10:45** both tell us that *"The Son of man (Jesus Christ) came not to be served but to serve, and to give His life as a ransom for many."* The preceding verse **(Matthew 20:27 and Mark 19:44)** both say that *"whosoever will be chief among you, let him be your servant..."*

There are legal duties and responsibilities placed upon us by the law, but there are also moral and ethical duties. There are actions that we should do and duties that we ought to perform. There are tasks and services that every Christian should be willing to engage in, because they are good, right and fitting. A servant of God should be willing to go beyond the letter of the law in doing good deeds to and for others. Jesus' first Sermon was a radical message to call His followers beyond the letter of the law to a higher calling on their life and ministry. In this Sermon He said that *"Ye have heard that it hath been said by them of old time..., But I say unto you..."* Jesus still has a fresh word for His followers today, and if we are able to hear His voice and the cry of those around us, we shall move out into ever broadening areas of ministry.

Our Christian duty is something required of us. We have an obligation. We "owe" our past, our present, and our posterity our very best to do all we can do and be all we can be. We must be willing, ready and able to share what we have and what we are when and where life demands. "We must pay our dues."

THE OBLIGATIONS:

We often forget our indebtedness. We are indeed indebted to the past for being where we are and for being what we are today. Each generation stands on the shoulders of the previous generation and each generation profits from those who have lived in previous generations and have made contributions, great or small. The church and the world of today are what they are because of the blood, sweat and tears of previous ages. What we know is a constant accumulation of the work and wisdom of the ages. Then we are also indebted and we have an obligation to the future, our posterity. We are responsible for receiving, adding to, and passing on the great body of knowledge, of information and revelation, which we have received so that the Church of Jesus Christ may continue to grow and develop.

We are required, bound, and compelled by a debt of gratitude to heed and respond to the demands placed on us by God and humanity. Out of our past there have been those who have felt this "pull from without" and because they responded to it as an obligation placed upon them, our valleys have not been as deep, our mountains and hills have not been so high, and our path has been made smooth and our way has been made straight.

There have been many unseen and unknown saints who have provided vital ministries in the lives of individual Christians and Christian churches. These ministries have met the needs of others and have fulfilled the will of God who commands us to show charity to others. There have been, and are, many Samaritans on life's road who have been there and have made a difference because of their sense of obligation.

THE CLAIM:

Finally we must realize, and never forget, that others have a claim on us. The most pitiful sight today is to walk or drive along our city streets and observe the many beggars. It is a statement and an indictment against our times to see that we have not resolved the issue of the "beggar." Jesus says that *"The poor you will always have with you..."* **(John 12:8)**. We can understand many of the existing reasons for some people in our society being poor. But for the poor to be put in a position of having to beg is a totally different condition. Jesus tells us to ask, not to beg to have our needs met. Beggars are an indication of a society grown cold and callous. Beggars are an indication of needs that have become demands. Beggars are an indication of the downward plight of the poor. Beggars are an indication of a society becoming more secular and less saintly. David could say, *"I have never seen the righteous' seed begging bread"* **(Psalm 37:25)**, because God's people were more compassionate during his day than they are in our day. I doubt whether that same statement can be made today.

The difference in David's day, and the reason for people not having to beg is that others were sensitive to the needs of the poor, and those who had gave to those who did not have. This was the Golden Rule, and this is the statement of claim placed on the Christian society. **Romans 15:1** tells us that *"We that are strong ought to bear the infirmities of the weak, and not to please ourselves."*

The Apostle Paul told the Galatians **(Galatians 6:2)** that they were to *"Bear ye one another's burdens, and so fulfil the law of Christ."* Our brothers and sisters have a claim on us. We are our brother's keepers. Jesus says in **Matthew 25th chapter** that He shall someday separate the righteous from the unrighteous based on how each person has heeded the "pull from without."

In **Acts 4:36** there was a man surnamed Barnabas (son of consolation) who sold his land and gave the proceeds to the apostles for distribution to the poor and needy. In **Acts 5:1ff.** there was a husband and wife (Ananias and Sapphire) who were great pretenders. They sold a possession and kept back a part of the selling price and lied about the transaction. There are those in Christian churches today who claim that they are giving to meet the needs of the poor, (and that they are tithing to the work of the ministry) and they are holding back in their missionary work and their ministry to God and humanity. Our tithe is not only monetary but we are called to give of our time, talent and treasure. Our obligation is a wholistic stewardship.

Our present age and the coming generation both have a claim on us. We cannot fail to answer or refuse to answer this demand of the ministry that is our duty and our obligation, for as often as we do good unto the least of our brothers and sisters, we are showing our love to Christ who loved us and gave His life for us.

CHAPTER 3

THE DESIRE OF THE MINISTRY

There are many demands placed upon the Christian by the circumstances in society. There are also many other pressures from outside the individual. These "pulls" and "pressures" from without must in some way be matched by the "push from within." We are not only "drawn" into the ministry by forces from without. We are also "driven" into the ministry, or into service, by the forces from within.

Herein lies our great concern. The desires or "push" within us can be motivated by "love" or by "lust." There is a thin line between what is "true" religion and what is fanatical zeal. The push from within can be caused by our love for God and humanity, or the push can be caused by our own selfish urges and desires.

There is a biblical account of a man called Simon who was converted from sorcery to Christianity. He was impressed with the Apostles Peter and John and their ability to perform miracles. He tried to give them money that he might acquire the power, that on whomsoever he lay hands, they might receive the Holy Ghost. Peter rebuked Simon stating that Simon's heart was not right in the sight of God (**Acts 8:9-24**). There are those today who are using the power of healing, deliverance, etc. in ways that are not pleasing to God. They are performing acts out of lust and for "filthy lucre" rather than out of love for God and humanity.

We must make every attempt to assess and evaluate our motives and our desires for being involved in Christian service. We must be sure that there is a genuine "call" to the Lord's service, and at the same time, we must be equally sure that our response to the call is also genuine.

There are certain basic drives which have been described by psychologists. These internal drives determine our actions and reactions to external factors. There is in each of us a desire to achieve, to be recognized and appreciated for who we are and what we do.

Jesus says that the first criteria for Christian discipleship and service is self-denial. He states that, *"If any man will come after Me, let him deny himself, and take up his cross daily, and follow Me"* **(Luke**

9:23). The Christian ministry entails not only self-sacrifice, but the Christian ministry also entails self-denial.

The motivation or impulse within us that answers the needs and demands around us is our love for Christ and our love for our fellows. In Mark's gospel Jesus was asked, *"...Which is the first commandment of all?"* His answer was, *"The first of all commandments is, Hear, O Israel; The Lord our God is one Lord: And thou shalt love the Lord thy God with all thy heart, and with all thy soul, and with all thy mind, and with all thy strength: this is the first commandment. And the second is like, namely this, Thou shalt love thy neighbor as thyself. There is none other commandment greater than these."* **(Mark 12:28-31)**.

The Apostle Paul also speaks of this Christian desire when he tells the Christians at Corinth that he and other Christian workers were constrained, (i.e., compelled, obliged) to perform their ministry by the love of Christ **(II Corinthians 5:14)**. We are called to have the heart, the nature and character of our Lord, Jesus Christ. To be born again is to receive the Spirit of love for God and for humanity. Jesus says that we are to love one another even as He loves us.

THE DEDICATION:

Those who would be involved in Christian service must have a sense of call, a sense of mission, and a sense of purpose. To live the life of a Disciple of Christ is to live a dedicated life. Christian ministry is a "high" or a "heavenly" calling. It is a sacred vocation. There are many warnings in Scripture that caution any person desiring to become a co-laborer with Christ to "count the cost." Historically the Christian Church has considered those who entered any aspect of service as being set apart by God. Also they are anointed by the Holy Spirit to enter into the work of the ministry. Our vocation is a sacred thing. It is a "summons" from God. We do not choose Him, but He chooses us.

In Chapters VIII and IX we will be looking at the distinctions and diversities of the ministry. Here, however, it needs to be said that in any area of Christian service, a major prerequisite for Christian ministry is total dedication. The demands form within and without are so great that anything less that a deep desire and wholehearted dedication will put the Christian worker at risk.

If the call is genuine, then the dedication will be adequate. God does not always call individuals who are totally prepared in all aspects for service. The good news is that God will equip those whom He calls. Any person who is willing to completely surrender his/her life into the hands of God will be shaped and molded according to God's will and for God's work. The history of the Scriptures is replete with examples of God working with, in and through ordinary persons to accomplish great and extra-ordinary tasks.

There must be dedication to the call, but there must also be dedication to the task and to the mission. God not only calls, He calls for a reason. A great and grave danger in Christian work is hearing the call and leaving without getting all of the directions for the duty placed upon us. When God commissions a person for a mission, or for a ministry, He also gives guidelines for the work. We must not only be dedicated to God's will and God's word. We must also be dedicated to God's work and God's way.

The first test confronting Jesus in His earthly ministry was whether He would attempt to work Satan's way, or if He would work God's way. The synoptic Gospels point out that our Lord Jesus Christ passed the test and chose God's way rather than Satan's way. Often we fail because we are overly ambitious, and we allow our desires to distort our thinking and allow our love for success to override our Love for our Savior. In so doing we fall for one of the temptations of Satan.

One of the most difficult tasks in Christian ministry is being able to wait patiently for our orders. Often we are anxious to get started on a venture because of the demands and needs we see all around us. There are times when we rush in to the rescue when the wisest action would be to not act, or to wait until we are instructed when, where and how to act. It has been stated that "fools rush in where angels fear to tread." Angels are those messengers who know how to wait on orders from their Commander, and then with the swiftness of a winged being, make haste to accomplish the God-given task.

To be on a mission is to be "sent." We must be able to trust the "Sender" who understands every aspect of the mission and who knows when, where, what, and how the mission is to be accomplished.

And then we must not only have a clear sense of call and mission, but we must have a sense of purpose. We are called to be agents and ambassadors more than to be instruments. An instrument or tool in the hand of another is a mindless extension of that hand. An agent, however, is aware and conscious of being used and conscious of the reason for being of service. God wants us to not only be involved in ministry, but He also wants us to be willing or desirous of providing a ministry and conscious of the ministry which we provide. We should not only understand what our ministry is, and where, when, and how we minister. We should also understand "why" we minister. God wants us to understand our purpose in life and our service to Him and humanity.

Dedication is not a blind, mindless service. We should realize our place in God's program and even though we only see "through a glass darkly," we should have at least a dim sense of God's aim and intent in using us. In knowing our purpose allows us to be more specific in our prayers to God and in our conversation with other ministers. When we understand our purpose in Christian service, we can begin to understand what the Scriptures mean when they say that we are to love the Lord our God "With all our mind."

After Jesus had spoken to the multitude in parables, he would take His twelve Disciples aside and explain to them the meaning of the parable. He would tell His Disciples, *"Unto you it is given to know the mystery of the Kingdom of God; but unto them that are without, all things are done in parables"* **(Mark 4:11)**. Christ has the same desire today, and that is that we are also aware and informed of His intention when he calls us and uses us in the ministry.

THE DETERMINATION:

To love God and love our service to Him and others, with all our mind, is to not only be dedicated but also to be determined. We must have a "made-up mind" to serve God and to serve this present age. We must be determined to allow nothing or no one to deter us from our mission and our ministry.

The great temptations and tests in our life of service will be aimed at turning us, stopping us, or slowing us in our assigned duty. We must be ever on the watch for pitfalls. There will be stumbling blocks in our pathway as we strive to be engaged in our ministry. Also there are hindrances that would impede us from completing our ministry.

The Scriptures are good at providing us with illustrations and examples of the many traps and tricks used by Satan to delay or deter us. There are pressures from the world, the flesh and the Devil which try our resolve to stay on course and complete our mission. **I John 2:16** warns us that we must be aware of the worldly desires that would hinder us, *"the lust of the flesh, the lust of the eyes, and the pride of life."* We must be driven by our love for God. We cannot be motivated by our love for the world, the lust of the flesh, or the lure of the Devil.

We must have a strong conviction that the task assigned to us can only be done by us. If we fail, the mission fails. We must make every attempt to complete our duty. The Apostle Paul says that we must *"Be steadfast, unmovable, always abounding in the work of the Lord, forasmuch as ye know that your labor is not in vain in the Lord"* (**I Corinthians 15:58**). At the end of his life, Paul was able to say with conviction *"I have fought a good fight, I have finished my course, I have kept the faith"* (**II Timothy 4:7**). Each of us must be determined to make this our testimony also.

THE DEVOTION:

The hallmark of the early church was that they devoted themselves to the teaching of the Apostles, the breaking of the bread, and to daily prayers. They were totally committed to the Lord and to one another. They had all things common. The Scriptures continually state that they were *"in one place and on one accord"*. Those who are called by God and who are sent to serve must be totally committed to their mission of ministry. They must also be committed to the mutual mission and ministry of others. We share in the duties, demands, and desires of other Christian workers.

There must be an affectionate spirit for service. This is the drive that gets the task completed. A Christian must have a healthy eagerness to do the will of God. We must say with the Apostle Paul in I

Corinthians 9:16, *"For necessity is laid upon me; yea, woe is unto me, if I preach not the gospel!"*

We all have the responsibility of acting and the necessity of giving an account for our actions. The Christian mandate is to *"Be ye doers of the word, and not hears only"* **(James 1:22)**. We are called and commissioned to do all according to the will of God and for the glory of God. We must be able and available for service. We must be true and loyal to our call to the ministry. A Christian is not only called to have "faith." We are also called to be "faithful."

If our society is failing today, it is because the churches are failing to be the "salt" of the earth and the "light" of the world. We can make a difference, but we can make a difference only when we are devoted to God and our world. We must be totally "sold out" to the ministry to which we have been assigned by God. We cannot take other's responsibility nor will we have to answer for other's faults and failures. We will, however, be called to give reason for our lack of devotion to our task. We can not take our talents and bury them, but we must use what we have to the best of our ability. All of our work will be tried when we stand before the "Judgment seat of Christ."

Every Christian is called to do all for God and for the building up of His Kingdom. Often we thing that working in the church and serving on committees and other positions are synonymous with working for God's Kingdom. Sometimes this is true. At other times we may be working against God's Program by doing "busy work" in the church. We must make every effort to realize where God is at work in our time. We must make a distinction between our programs and God's Program. God calls us outside of our local church and without the gates of the city to minister to those who are without the church congregation. Often we are called to launch out into the deep, to unknown areas, to perform and fulfill our ministry.

We cannot allow any other plan, program or purpose to interfere with God's plan and our high calling of ministry. There are many voices and many pseudo-religious endeavors which distract us from doing the will of God. When we live a devoted life and spend time in devotion, prayer and meditation, we will be directed in the most appropriate way of service. There are many temptations in our day which seem to be good because they are successful. There are many voices calling us to engage in new and exciting ways of providing for the needs of people in the church and in the world. But we are told to *"believe not every spirit, but try the spirits, whether they are of God: because false prophets are gone out into the world"* **(I John 4:1)**.

THE DYNAMIC:

The power behind our desire, dedication, determination and devotion is the Holy Spirit. Over and over again Jesus reminds the first Disciples of the "Promise of the Father." We too need to be reminded of the Promise and the Power of the Holy Spirit which is available for us to fully realize our mission of ministry. We fail and fail miserably to perform our tasks of service when we allow only our human desire to motivate us for service. When we are motivated by our own human desires, or by the desires of others, we will be unstable and unpredictable. Then our own feelings will determine who we are and what we do, rather that our attitude and actions being determined by our faith in God.

One of the saddest pictures in biblical history is that of Samson being tricked to attempt a great feat without the accompaniment of God. **Judges 16:20-21** says, *"And he [Samson] awoke out of his sleep, and said, I will go out as at other times before, and shake myself. And he wist (knew) not that the LORD was departed from him. But the Philistines took him, and put out his eyes, and brought him down to Gaza, and bound him with fetters of brass; and he did grind in the prison house."*

The biblical lesson here is that there is grave danger in going out to fight against evil in one's own strength and without the Presence and Power of the Holy Spirit. Samson was half-blind in his attempt to prove his own power. He allowed false pride and a wrong desire to influence his action. Too late he realized the foolishness of his ways. His last prayer according to several biblical translations was that God might *"Please strengthen me one more time, so that I may pay back the Philistines for the loss of at least one of my eyes."* The Philistines had put out one of Samson's eyes, but pride and self-conceit had already half-blinded Samson before he was captured.

We must never forget that while "love" is the motivating factor in

Christian ministry, the Holy Spirit is the motivating fact. The story of Samson is written for an example and for our edification that we might not succumb to the same temptation of going out in our own strength. Isaiah promises that *"Even the youths shall faint and be weary, and the young men shall utterly fall: But they that wait upon the LORD shall renew their strength; they shall mount up with wings as eagles; they shall run, and not be weary; and they shall walk, and not faint."* **(Isaiah 40:30-31)**

The driving force from within us is the Holy Spirit, The Spirit of Christ which equips us for ministry and then sends us forth with power. We are "pushed" from within by God's power as we are "pulled" from without by humanity's plight and God's Program. As we dedicate ourselves to God's will, he will give us increasingly greater works to do for Him. As our ministries increase, so will our power to perform our tasks. Our lives will become a dynamic force for change in the times in which we live.

CHAPTER 4

THE DISCOVERY OF THE MINISTRY

Even as there are many significant medical cures, technologies and scientific facts that have not been found out, there are many saints in churches who have never been discovered as to their gifts, talents, skills or latent aptitudes and abilities. Our churches are veritable gold mines of possibilities of service and ministries which can be used to the glory of God.

Each church must discover and develop a strategy for employing, equipping and empowering Christian ministers. One reason the "laborers are few" today in the field of mission is because we have no plan or program for "equipping the saints for the work of ministry." Another reason laborers are few is because we have no plan or program for discovering those in our churches who have buried talents.

We must devise a means of determining the needs, the demands of our society. We must also seek out those in our congregation who have the desire to serve. When Israel was seeking a king, Scriptures tell us that Saul was hiding among the "stuff." **(I Samuel 10:22)**. There are also those in our congregation who are stuck behind the "stuff" that hinders and hampers their ability to serve. Sometimes the "stuff" is theirs, and sometimes the "stuff" is ours. Their fears, doubts, lack of training, etc. cause them to hide from service. Then our own fears, doubts, envy, jealousy, lack of understanding cause us to keep them in hiding. Sins of omission and commission greatly limit the growth of the church and its ministry.

Often those who could be of great service to God's Program are in hiding because they have not been informed, instructed, taught or trained. in the many areas of their ministry. There is as great need today, as there has always been, to resolve the issues of selecting men and women for Christian service.

There is also a need to enable each Christian to discover their calling and determine where God has His hand on their lives. Men and women must evaluate their areas of time, talent and treasure, and determine how they might use these in service to God and humanity.

Churches can also diagnose their present needs for ministry and that of their community through surveys, questionnaires, and interviews. Individuals can determine their calling to the Christian ministry through prayer, group discussion, and dialogue with their pastor, or some senior member of the body of Christ. This does not have to be a member of the person's particular church, but one who is close to God and understands God's will. Open discussion, evaluation and even times of confrontation will create opportunities for disclosure and discovery of hidden resources within a congregation.

DISCOVERY MEANS TO BE AWAKE TO OUR MISSION OF MINISTRY:

The problem with many congregations and individual Christians is that they are unconscious, or asleep, to the need of Christian service and their ability or potential for service. There are those who are completely out of touch with the realities around them. We are living in the age of the "Information Superhighway" and the "World Wide Web," and yet there are those who are not conscious of the realities of life. Many in our churches today are uninformed and uninitiated when it comes to things of eternal value. They know a lot of "facts" about their religion but they know little of the great "truths" of their Faith.

In both the Old Testament and the New Testament there is often the alarm sounded for God's people to awaken from their sleep. There are grave dangers in being asleep when evil forces are active all around us. The demands today for people of good will is to awaken and become aware of the facts of life.

The Church must devise ways and means of quickening its members and encouraging each other in this vital area. Bible study and prayer will stir the consciousness and alert individuals to the call to duty and discipleship. It is very easy to become lulled to sleep by the many forces in our society. There are times when even religion can become a sedation and cause us to fail in some needed activity.

The first Disciples were often found sleeping when they should have been awake. Jesus would reprimand them for not being awake and for not "watching." We too must be alert and watch as well as pray. Religious exercises are not enough. We must be on our guard for opportunities of service. When we awaken to the "pull" from without (the needs within our communities) we will be also made conscious of our own opportunity to serve and to assist in meeting those needs. Paul says in **Romans 13:11**, *"And that, knowing the time, that now it is high time to awake out of sleep: for now is our salvation nearer than when we believed."*

God has a purpose for every life and the great discovery in life is to awaken to our own specific purpose in life and ministry. To be conscious of the social and spiritual conditions of our time can be depressing. To be informed of the causes of our problems and predicament can be informative and educational. But to be conscious of the cures which can be worked out through us as ministers of reconciliation will be exciting.

DISCOVERY MEANS BEING AWARE OF OUR MISSION OF MINISTRY:

It is one thing to be awake to the need of ministry, it is another thing to be aware of our own opportunity to serve and to provide a particular ministry. We must not only be conscious; we must also be cognizant of God's will for our lives. We cannot be half awake, but we must rise from our apathy and lethargy. We must become alert to our place and purpose in God's Program. We must be energized by our high calling to serve God and humanity.

To fully discover our ministry, we must be fully informed. We can not be dull and listless, nor can we be ignorant and oblivious to the state of affairs in our present age. We must use the media without allowing the media to use us. We must read, watch, and listen with understanding. The task of the minister is to be selective in becoming informed of events of the day. We must understand the manipulative attempts of others to mis-inform or mis-direct our minds. There is a battle for the mind which shall continue to the end of this present age. We can not stop the battle but we can engage in the struggle. To begin the struggle we must take charge of our own minds and our own thinking.

The Apostle Paul says in **Philippians 2:5** that we should *"Let this mind be in you, which was also in Christ Jesus..."* To the Roman Christians (**Romans 12:2**) he says *"Be not conformed to this world, but* *be ye transformed by the renewing of your mind, that ye may prove what is that good, and acceptable, and perfect, will of God."* When Jesus quotes the first commandment from **Deuteronomy 6:5**, He says that we must love God not only with all of our heart, and soul, and strength (might), but that we must also love God with all our mind. Often we fail to realize and understand that our Christian faith is not based solely on matters of the spirit but also on wisdom, knowledge and understanding.

The Scriptures often chide us against being "ignorant." This simply tells of the danger of "not knowing". We have often heard it said, "What you don't know won't hurt you." I am sure that the aging and maturing process will quickly dispel that tale, because much of the hurts we experience comes from finding out too little too late. We often suffer greatly from ignorance. The better informed we become, the better we are able to work for God. When we discover "truth" we also discover our task. When we learn God's will for our lives, we also learn God's work for our life's ministry.

There are those who speak of God's "permissive" will, not realizing that God is always active and involved. Our problem is that we are not cognizant of where, when, and how God is working. Often we are not alert or aware to what God is doing. We fail to become involved because we believe that He is not involved. Jesus tells those who chastised Him for working on the Sabbath that *"My Father worketh hitherto, and I work"* **(John 5:17)**. Another translation says *"My Father is still working, and so am I."* The Christian Church has become permissive because it believes that God is permissive. It is not that God allows things to happen or not happen. We allow things to be as they are because we fail through prayer and study to be informed of the Word of God and the work of God. We are called to be involved in the work of God even as Christ was involved. We know that God is at work in all things for good, to those who love Him and those who are called by Him **(Romans 8:28)**. We are therefore called to take up our cross daily and follow Christ in the work-plan of God.

DISCOVERY MEANS ACKNOWLEDGEMENT OF OUR MISSION OF MINISTRY:

Ministry begins when we say "YES" To God's call on our life.

This call is a very practical event. Often we make God's call mystical and spiritual when in reality it is personal and practical. When we are able to respond in a personal and practical manner to the call, our ministry has begun. There are those who are apt to place so much philosophical concepts and nebulous ideas to our desire to do ministry that we become confused and afraid to say "yes" to God. There have been, there are, and there will be many individuals called by God and yet are inactive because of bad advise from others.

There are those who refuse and refute the call of God. Those who refuse the call often do so because they have failed to take the earlier steps of becoming awake and aware of God in their lives. Being asleep or half asleep, they are not conscious of who God is when He calls them. Their state of mind or condition of being is of such that they do not recognize the call as coming from God. We find those in the Scriptures who were not conscious of God's call. They contributed the call to natural factors or to the call of some human voice. In **I Samuel 3:1-10** we are told that God was calling Samuel but Samuel thought that the call was coming from Eli, the priest.

Then there are those who refute the call of God. They can not acknowledge the call because they have been told that they are not worthy or not ready to serve God. There are many saints who have waited all of their lives to get ready for God's call. If God calls a man or woman for service, He will also prepare them for that service. The only ability we need when God calls us is "availability." We must trust God to prepare us to do His will and complete His work. **Philippians 1:6** says *"Being confident of this very thing, that He which hath begun a good work in you will perform it until the day of Jesus Christ."*

By faith we believe and acknowledge that if God calls us, that call is a gift from God and with the gift of ministry comes the gift of Power. When we discover our call to ministry, we also discover an amazing paradox. **Philippians 2:11c-12** says, *"Work out your own salvation with fear and trembling. For it is God which worketh in you both to will and to do of His good pleasure."* This is the mystery of our faith. This is the Christian paradox. We are to work as though our ministry depended totally on us. Yet we are to trust and pray as though our ministry depended totally on God.

We must seek the help, counsel and guidance of other Christians but yet we can not allow others to dissuade us from our assigned task. God is faithful in that if He has a call on our lives He will make it plain in time. We can not act in haste. We must exercise patience and allow time for God's plan and purpose for our life to unfold. On the other hand we cannot procrastinate regarding our call.

DISCOVERY MEANS ACCEPTING OUR MISSION OF MINISTRY:

The greatest step of discovering God's call is that of acceptance. This is more than just to say yes, but it is to step out on our conviction. It is to place our life into the hand of God. **John 1:12** tells us that *"As many as received Him, to them gave He power to become the sons of God..."* Acceptance is our willingness to receive Him who has been willing to receive us as sons and daughters. Acceptance is saying "yes" to Him who has said "yes" to us.

Even today there are those who reject the Master and His ministry. There are those who will not allow Christ to have a place in their lives. They refuse to acknowledge God's claim on their lives, and they refuse to acknowledge their responsibility to God and their responsibility to and for others.

Discovery means arriving at a point in life of accepting our purpose for being of service to God and others. Once we can admit to ourselves that we live to help others live, and we become aware of the fact that we serve God as we serve humanity, we have started on the road to spiritual as well as social growth and development.

Discovery is also becoming aware of the fact that to be accepting of God's call is not necessarily to have a life that is totally acceptable. The Prophet Isaiah was willing to be involved in God's Program. He accepted the call but he also realized that he was not acceptable. He knew that although he was called to minister to a people, he was also "one of them". He was a man of "unclean lips." When he was able to accept God and God's call on his life, then God was able to make Isaiah acceptable. **(Isaiah 6)**

Although God has a plan for each of our lives, we can not know that plan until we say "yes" to the call, admit our shortcomings, and allow God to equip us and make us acceptable for service. We must also realize that *"we have this treasure in earthen vessels, that the excellency of the power may be of God, and not of us"* **(II Corinthians 4:7)**.

DISCOVERY MEANS ASCERTAINING OUR MISSION OF MINISTRY:

II Timothy 2:15 tells us that we are to, *"Study to shew thyself approved unto God, a workman that needeth not to be ashamed, rightly dividing the word of truth."* This was the Apostle Paul's charge to young Timothy in the first century. The charge is no less pertinent to those of us living in the twentieth century. We must make every effort to not only be accepted but also to be approved by God. We need His stamp and seal of approval.

Our task is to make every effort to grow in body, soul and spirit. There are many things which appear to be concealed, veiled, hidden or withheld from us. Yet things have a way of becoming plain to those who are willing to go a little further, to try a little longer, to dig a little deeper. Jesus said, *"Ask, and it shall be given you; seek, and ye shall find; knock, and it shall be opened unto you: For every one that asketh receiveth; and he that seeketh findeth; and to him that knocketh it shall be opened"* **(Matthew 7:7-8)**.

This is one of the great promises of Scripture. God's Word promises that there is nothing hidden that shall not be revealed **(Matthew 10:26)**. We often fail to ascertain the breadth, length, depth and height of our ministry because we do not claim the great promises and possibilities given to us by God.

We must devise a means and method of getting to know what God is doing in our world and in our lives. We must understand that the veil has been rent between ourselves and the Holy of Holies and we can approach the mysteries with boldness and confidence. There are exciting discoveries regarding ourselves and our world waiting to show themselves to us. We must not seek knowledge simply for the sake of being knowledgeable, but we must seek knowledge, nevertheless, to be able to fulfill our ministry.

Jesus' great invitation to men and women down through the ages still hold true and relevant. *"Come unto me, all ye that labor and are heavy laden, and I will give you rest. Take my yoke upon you, and learn of Me; for I am meek and lowly in heart: and ye shall find rest unto your souls. For My yoke is easy, and My burden is light."* **(Matthew 11:28-30)**. When we discover Christ we discover ourselves, and when we learn of our Lord and Savior Jesus Christ, we also learn from Him.

THE MANY WAYS OF DISCOVERY:

Once we awaken and become aware of the forces within us and the factors around us which create our sense of ministry, there are numerous ways and means of ascertaining the deeper meaning of our call. From the human side of things we can list many aids to further understand our gift of ministry. Here are at least ten such aids. These are not listed in any order of priority but may happen or not happen during the discovery process.

Information: To become informed is to allow something to take shape or to take form within our minds. One of the early phases of discovery is to allow the concept to develop into something we are able to grasp and understand. There is a period of incubation and germination when our immature thoughts and feelings begin to take on flesh and sinew. Information can be acquired through study, experience or instruction.

Instruction: We must be open to those who have the education and the ability to impart knowledge to others. We must realize that there is no service or ministry which has not been performed by someone in the past. We must be willing, ready and able to accept the teaching and leadership of others. A good minister is a good disciple, or follower.

Education: The learning process is not only receiving instruction but it is also drawing out of ourselves untapped knowledge. We must allow ourselves to become totally open to all aspects of learning. There are times when we surprise ourselves with our latent possibilities.

Stimulation: We are motivated by the thoughts and ideas of others. Learning and growing in groups facilitate our growth and development. Often we are made aware of where and how God is working in our lives by listening to the testimony of others.

Participation: There is power in groups and cooperate ventures. We find on the one hand that when we participate in a cause we become more identified with that cause. Non-involvement on the other hand causes us to lose interest and desire. The more we put into a thing, or the greater our investment the greater our returns. The more we give the more we receive.

Cooperation: Often when we work along with others we are drawn to a greater degree than when we "go it" alone. God's word tells us that one can chase a thousand, but two will put ten thousand to flight. **(Deuteronomy 32:30)** There is no limit to what we can discover when we join together.

Orientation: Before we can make the proper discoveries in ministry or in life, we must be facing the right direction. We must align or position ourselves so that the truth might be seen. It is possible to have our face turned away from that which would enlighten us. We can become involved in false ideas and false ideologies and be totally misled. We will find it hard to discover the truth if we are confronted with falsehood.

Investigation: The Prophet Isaiah challenges us to *"Seek ye the LORD while he may be found, call ye upon Him while He is near..."* **(Isaiah 55:6)**. We can not take things at face value, but we must be willing to dig and look beneath the surface.

Analysis: Often to see things more clearly we must take them apart and examine them more carefully. Many individuals become involved in false religions and improper causes because they do not take the time or spend the effort to analyze the facts. We must diagnose every situation to decide whether it is true or whether it is true for us. We must not only look at all of the facets of a situation but we must also identify what that situation really means.

<u>**Synthesis**</u>: Not only must we be able to take things apart and investigate them, but in order to discover the facts of our ministry we must also be able to put things together. Often we must arrange and rearrange things in ways that make the most sense for us. This could mean that we will have to do research often into the particular issue and also to study the history in an attempt to fully understand.

All of these ways work together to assist us and equip us for the work of ministry and for the discovery of God's call to us. To discover God's will for our lives is serious business. It is also a conscious effort on our part to inform ourselves of our mission and ministry in God's service. We must, therefore, learn to use every means at our disposal, which is within the will of God, to understand our place in His Kingdom and our purpose in His service.

CHAPTER 5

THE DISCERNMENT OF THE MINISTRY

Crucial to the call into the Christian ministry is having the ability to see, to discern, and to distinguish between the will of God and the will, or wants, or wishes of human beings. There is a need in the church today to have the mental capacity to distinguish and discriminate in making moral judgments regarding the work and the workers in the body of Christ. Much harm can be done by not taking the time and making decisions carefully when choosing those who are being assigned to Christian ministry. Also there must be care and caution taken to assure that once a person has been assigned to a task or ministry, what is done and how it is done by that person is in keeping with God's will, God's way, and God's word.

It has been said that Christianity is not only "taught" but it is also "caught." It can also be said that we understand our Christian ministry not only by what we are able to discover but also what we are able to discern.

I Corinthians 2:14 tells us that *"The natural (unspiritual) man receiveth not the things of the Spirit of God: for they are foolishness unto him: neither can he know them, because they are spiritually discerned."* As Christians, we must be open not only to information about God's word, but we must also be open to revelation from God. **Romans 8:14** tells us *"For as many as are led by the Spirit of God, they are the sons of God."*

There are things which we are able to discover through the many means found in Chapter IV, (The Discovery Of The Ministry) of this book. There are also other possible ways and means of acquiring wisdom and knowledge. But in truth, God's Word tells us that *"The fear of the Lord is the beginning of wisdom: a good understanding have all they that do His commandments."* **(Psalm 111:10)**

THE GIFT OF DISCERNMENT:

First, there are things which come to us as gifts in life. **James 1:17** says, *"Every good gift and every perfect gift is from above, and cometh* *down from the Father of lights, with whom is no variableness, neither shadow of turning."*

In Chapter III, (The Desire Of The Ministry) of this book we speak of the Holy Spirit as "Power." In this Chapter we see the Holy Spirit not only as Power but also as "Guide." Jesus promises in **John 15:13** that *"When He, the Spirit of truth, is come, He will guide you in all truth: for He shall not speak of Himself; but whatsoever He shall hear, that shall He speak: and He will shew you things to come."*

This promise of Christ is that we shall be given illumination, inspiration and revelation as a "gift" by the Holy Spirit. There are things for which we must stride. Then, there are things which come to us as a gift from our Heavenly Guide.

We are given illumination into the mysteries of life and the realities of living. Christianity is not only a faith that generates "heat" but it also generates "light." We not only have the stimulation and excitement of our faith, but we have a Spirit of discernment which enlightens our mind. Deep issues of life are disclosed to us which, without the guidance of the Holy Spirit would pass our ability to discover or find out. Even in our present day, through dreams and visions, God still speaks to His children and to His Church.

Through prayer we are not only able to talk to God, but also through prayer God is able to talk to us. Prayer is two-way communication. It is a dialogue with the Divine. Prayer is a way in which we are able to discern the will of God for our lives. Meditation opens us up to the mind of God. When we are able to ruminate on God's Word, we are carried to a deeper level of understanding. We are able *"to comprehend with all saints what is the breadth, and length, and depth, and height; and to know the love of Christ which passeth knowledge"* **(Ephesians 3:18-19a)**.

The New Testament often speaks of the mysteries of the Faith. Paul says in **I Corinthians 4:1** that ministers of Christ are stewards of the mysteries of God. In the Old Testament the Prophet Daniel says that *"There is a God in heaven that revealeth secrets..."* **(Daniel 2:28)**.

There are aspects of life which are uncovered when we least expect them. Moses had tended sheep for forty years and had never discovered the burning bush until God decided to make Himself known to him in a bush that burned but was not consumed. We too may spend years in mundane situations until God decides to reveal His mysteries to us. For various reasons we may have to wait for the vision. Sometimes we are not ready for the disclosure. Sometimes the moment is not right for the disclosure. We must realize that God does not work according to our time table but in His own time and according to His own plan and program.

God also inspires us towards discernment. He creates in us an excitement which opens us up to new vistas and new visions. David prayed for this inspiration when he asked God to *"Create in me a clean heart, O God; and renew a right spirit within me. Restore unto me the joy of Thy salvation; and uphold me with Thy free spirit"* **(Psalm 51:10-12)**. This type of inspiration opens us up to the mysteries and discoveries of true Christian ministry. It was this inspiration which moved those heroes of faith to accomplish great things for God, and it is the same motivational factor which will energize our mission of ministry, and stretch our scope of sacred service.

Paul says in **Acts 16th Chapter** that after he had seen the vision, immediately he, Timothy, Luke and Silas endeavoured to go into Macedonia. They were assured that the Lord had called them to preach to those in that country. When they arrived in Macedonia, there was a woman named Lydia whose heart had already been opened by God to discern and receive the message of Paul, Silas, Timothy and Luke. Lydia also discerned that God had a ministry for her. She led her household to Christ and opened that house as a house of Christian worship. This is the first reality of discernment. We are enabled to understand God's will not by might nor by power but discernment as a gift from God through His Holy Spirit.

THE GLEANINGS OF DISCERNMENT:

The second reality of discernment is that there are things which are gleaned in the discovery of our service to God. True there are gifts, but there are times when we must expend some energy to receive these gifts. We must do as **Ruth** did in the Bible. We must go out into the field and glean for those blessings which otherwise might go unnoticed or unused. The paradox of our Christian ministry is that we must wait and trust as though everything depends on God. At the same time we must work and toil as though everything depends on us. It is only when we are willing, ready and able to do our part as well as when we are open and accepting of God doing His part that our ministry really becomes whole.

When Jesus had fed the multitude, He told His disciples to gather up the fragments that remain, that nothing be lost. **(John 6:12)**. We too must learn to not only seek the gifts but also to realize the gleanings. We often become concerned only about the "big" blessings, the "big" churches, the "big" programs and fail to gather up the fragments.

We must exercise our gift of discernment to observe where we might be able to go and serve on some insignificant mission field as well as in some great metropolis. In being fishers of men we must be willing to throw out our nets for the "minnows" as well as for the "game" fish.

In discerning, we must be able to discriminate between things which are good and things which are godly. We must discern where God is at work in the world and make haste and join Him. We must learn how to make a distinction where God makes a difference. It is only when we are led by the Holy Spirit that we are able to receive divine guidance. It will be there and there only that we are able to receive the gifts and gleanings from God.

As we seek to discover and develop our ministry, we must be able to understand and use all of our mental and spiritual faculties in ways that will assist our discernment of God's will in our lives. Some of the ways we are able to glean for wisdom and to gain the right understanding are as follows:

HELPS TO DISCERNMENT:

JUDGMENT: We are often told in scripture that we are not to "judge." We are also cautioned by others not to be judges. Because we misunderstand the reason for Christ's warning and the purpose of this word of caution in scripture, we give the wrong advice. By mis-interpretation and mis-application, we fail to apply the mental power and ability of judgment in ways that would enhance our ministry. "Judgment" is the ability to distinguish between two given concepts as they relate to a common object or idea. We must have the power and ability to ascertain the facts, while knowing that facts are not truths but only observations. We must consciously seek to have the mind of Christ in order to value and evaluate things using divine judgment and discernment.

The Apostle Paul tells the Christians at Corinth **(I Corinthians 6:2-3)**, *"Do ye not know that the saints shall judge the world? and if the world shall be judged by you, are ye unworthy to judge the smallest matters? Know ye not that ye shall judge angels? how much more things that pertain to this life?"* As Christians and as the Church of Christ, we have an awesome responsibility. The only way in which we will be able to fulfill our task is to seek the gift and ability to discern matters pertaining to our mission and the ministry in and through the Church.

I Thessalonians 5:21 tells us to *"Prove (test) all things; hold fast that which is good."* We are expected to be inspectors. As the Christian Church we are called to be "fruit inspectors." Paul tells us in **Galatians 5:22-23** how to distinguish one who belongs to Christ by the fruit of love, joy, peace, longsuffering, gentleness, goodness, faith, meekness, and temperance. We must be able to judge where there is good fruit, bad fruit and no fruit. We are known by the fruit we bear.

WISDOM: To accurately and adequately discern we must be wise in the word of God. **Hebrews 4:12** tells us *"For the word of God is quick, and powerful, and sharper than any two-edged sword, piercing even to the dividing asunder of soul and spirit, and of the joints and marrow, and is a discerner of the thoughts and intents of the heart."* **Psalm 119:104-105** says *"Through Thy precepts (teachings) I get understanding... Thy word is a lamp unto my feet, and a light unto my path."*

Wisdom is applied knowledge, and spiritual wisdom is rightly interpreting and applying the word of God. Great wisdom must be used in choosing those who will provide ministry within the Body of Christ. In **Acts 1:24** we are told that when the disciples needed to select a person to take the place of Judas, they *"prayed, and said Thou, Lord,* *which knowest the hearts of all men, shew whether of these two Thou hast chosen..."* Peter was wise enough to recall God's word from the book of **Psalms** and to seek God's will in their decision.

DISCRIMINATION: There is a thin line between right and wrong and between good and evil. It is incumbent upon the people of God to use discernment in distinguishing between those things which are in the will of God and those things which are the will of man. We must train our spirit to "see" where God is working in the life of the individual and in the collective life of the Church. **Matthew 13:14** repeats the caution from **Isaiah 6:9-10** that "By hearing ye shall hear, and shall not understand; and seeing ye shall see, and shall not perceive."

HINDRANCES TO DISCERNMENT:

We often fail to discern and discriminate due to our own short-sightedness and moral blindness in matters of determining right and wrong. Many of our choices are based on our nearsightedness and our failure to open our eyes to reality. Conditions which limit our ability to "see" or discern are:

DARKNESS: We often fail to perceive things because we are not enlightened. We often work in the dark and then wonder why we are not able to see. Before we can reason properly we must have the light of God's word to illuminate our mind. **Psalm 119:105** says that God's word is *"a lamp unto my feet, and a light unto my path."* We are hindered in coming to the truth when we deny God's word. Our Lord Jesus Christ says that He is the Light of the World, and when we follow Him as His disciples we will be able to discern right from wrong and good from evil.

DISTORTION AND DECEPTION: Often we are blind to reality due to the clouds of doubt, prejudice, fear, hatred, pride and passion. Any of these conditions cast a cloud before us which limit our ability to perceive things as they really are. Paul says that we see through a glass darkly (**I Corinthians 13:12**). Even at our best we are not able to comprehend the ways of God who "moves in a mysterious way." When we further compound out reasoning by any of the conditions listed above, we become truly blind and unable to discern God's will.

DISTANCE: Often we are too far from the situation to comprehend the realities or to discern the facts adequately. Often we are also too far from God to be shown the things we need to know to assess the situation. Often there are persons and things that come between us and limit our ability to discern. Jesus warns His disciples that until they were able to forsake father, mother, wife, children, brother, and self, they could not be His disciples **(Luke 14:26)**.

Much can be said regarding the helps and hindrances that impact our ability to discern God's will and God's word. These few areas are listed to assist us in realizing the need for discernment and the forces that limit our abilities.

CHAPTER 6

THE DESIGN OF MINISTRY

Our God is a God of order and organization. Even before the foundations of the world, God had a plan and program for our creation, justification, salvation and final glorification. **Ephesians 1:4-6** states that, *"According as He hath chosen us in Him before the foundation of the world, that we should be holy and without blame before Him in love: Having predestinated us unto the adoption of children by Jesus Christ to Himself, according to the good pleasure of His will, To the praise of the glory of His grace, wherein He hath made us accepted in the Beloved."*

Paul states in **Romans 8:28** *"And we know that all things work together for good to them that love God, to them who are the called according to His purpose. For whom He did foreknow, He also did predestinate to be conformed to the image of His Son, that He might be the firstborn among many brethren. Moreover whom He did predestinate, them He also called: and whom He called, them He also justified: and whom He justified, them He also glorified."*

God is the divine Architect, the designer of the universe. If we are made in His image and likeness, and if we are true followers (disciples) of His Son, Jesus Christ, then we too must do all things decently and in order **(I Corinthians 14:40)**. We are called to be change agents, transforming chaos and disorder into concord and order. We are called to change darkness into light and to bring freshness to that which has become corrupt, because we are the "Salt" of the earth and the "Light" of the world **(Matthew 5:13-14)**. Christ is the Light of the world, and we are called to let our light shine that others might see our good works and glorify our Father which is in heaven **(Matthew 5:16)**.

THE PLAN:

First, the plan or design we use must be biblical. If God is a God of design and we are made in God's image and likeness, then we must follow God's word, God's will, God's way, when we start out to do

God's work. We can not conduct God's business according to our desire or according to the ways of the world.

Through prayer and study, we must strive to know the word of God. We must look at the needs, the problems, the conditions around us. Then we must seek to not only see the situation but we must also have an understanding of the situation. We must turn to God in prayer and study to see and hear from His word what He would have us to do. God has an answer to every problem. The prophetic task today, is as it has been down through the ages; to say "What wilt Thou have me to do?"

God has an answer to all of our questions, and God has a solution to all of our problems. Even before we begin to see the problem, God already has the outcome available for us. Even before we get into a situation God has a way planned to get us out of the situation.

I Corinthians 10:13 says, *"There hath no temptation taken you but such as is common to man; but God is faithful, who will not suffer you to be tempted above that ye are able; but will with the temptation also make a way to escape, that ye may be able to bear it."* Paul tells us in **Romans 8:28** that *"...we know that all things work together for good to them that love God, to them who are the called according to His purpose."* This is the good news of the Gospel, that in everything God works with us for good.

This is not only true regarding temptations, but it also applies to every test and every trial. When we allow ourselves to be led and guided by the Holy Spirit, we will be able to ascertain God's will and God's way through and out of any situation. David was able to say *"Yea, though I walk through the valley of the shadow of death, I will fear no evil: for Thou art with me; Thy rod and Thy staff they comfort me"* **(Psalm 23:4)**.

Our plan must not only follow God's word, but also His will and His way. We must seek to know God's desire (His will) for us and for our lives. It takes more than Bible reading to know what God has planned for us. We must meditate on every aspect of our Christian life and ascertain what God is doing in His divine plan to get glory out of our life and out of our Christian service.

Second, the plan or design for our life should be creative. God is a God of excitement and surprises. God often has new ways of doing things with new people and in new times and places. We must be open to change. Although God achieved certain things in certain ways in the past does not mean that he will achieve those same things in the same way in the present or in the future. In every age and in every dispensation God still says, *"Behold I will do a new thing"* **(Isaiah 43:19)**.

When we read the Bible we discover that God did things in one particular way or fashion on several occasions. Then we later discover another prophet through whom God does things in what seems to be a radical way. God's ways are not like our ways nor His thoughts like our thoughts **(Isaiah 55:8-9)**. **Hebrews 1:1** says, *"God, who at sundry (various) times and in divers (different) manners (ways) spake in time past unto the fathers by the prophets, hath in these days spoken unto us by His Son, whom He hath appointed heir of all things, by whom also He made the worlds..."*

We must be open to being innovative and imaginative. I know that there are inherent dangers in being imaginative, but when we allow the Spirit of God to inform, lead and direct our thoughts, we will be able to create new and exciting plans. God may still have surprises in store for us, and you, dear reader might be that person through whom God will do a new thing.

In making plans, we should take the time to allow God to enter into our planning session. **Matthew 18:19** says, *"...if two of you shall agree on earth as touching any thing that they shall ask, it shall be done for them of My Father which is in heaven."* We often use this Scripture to speak of worship or church disputes. While this might be very true, Jesus might also mean that when we come together to plan in small groups or as the church collectively, God's Spirit will also be present to instruct and guide us. The Holy Spirit is the unseen member of every planning session. Our problem is that we make Him a "guest" and an "outsider", rather than letting Him take His true position as Chairman of the Board.

Third, the plan and design for our life service must be purposeful. God is not in the business of assigning "busy" work to His ministers.

Every task fits into the ultimate will and plan of God. In God's economy, there are no big "I's" and little "You's." We all have a place in kingdom building and there are no ranks or divisions. God is the Chief Administrator, and the "buck" stops with Him. We have divided and sub-divided the work of the ministry, but that is not God's doing.

When we are called by God to become engaged in His service, we must ask the question, "Lord, what will you have me to do?" Before we begin to make plans regarding our ministry, we must first determine God's purpose for our ministry. We must discover "what" before we can discover "how."

Our plans must be oriented towards God and designed according to His will and purpose. We must be able to always say, *"Lord, not my will, but Thy will be done."* **(Luke 22:42)**. Our ministry must be done with intentionality but it must be God's intention for us rather than our intention for our ministry. Our will, our work, and our way must be acceptable unto God.

Often we limit God's work through us because we work towards secondary purposes while God wants us to work towards primary goals. God has a great plan for His world. Often we only think about our ministry, our church, our city, our country, our race, our religion and our time. While we are being exclusive in our service, God has universal plans for all eternity.

Fourth, our plan and design for our ministry must be pertinent. We must "serve this present age" rather than to be trapped in the past or stymied by the future. Jesus warned the first disciples, and He warns us today in **Matthew 6:34** to, *"Take therefore no thought for tomorrow for the morrow shall take thought for the things of itself. Sufficient unto the day is the evil thereof."* The Apostle Paul says in **Philippians 4:13** that we must forget those things which are behind.

Our plans must be related to those things which are germane to the time, place and purpose for which we have been called and to which we render service. We can not try to fit square pegs into round holes. We must match the ministry with the mission. God is very adept in sending the right person to the right place to do the right job. When God calls, we must make sure that we are the ones He is calling. In some ways it is good to respond too slowly than to react too quickly.

Even as the disciples asked the question "Lord, is it I" when Christ said that one of them would betray Him; we must also ask the same question when there is a task to be performed.

THE PRECEPTS:

In every good design there are basic rules, roles, regulations and responsibilities which govern the way we start and proceed in an endeavor. There are biblical principles, and there are also secular philosophies which have proven to be true. We must pray for wisdom, knowledge and understanding in order to meet the requirements of our task. We must be open to the sharing of others and the support from those who have already traveled the path upon which we are preparing to embark. And then we too must understand and be able to share our understanding with others.

Paul says that the pastor must be "apt" to teach. It is interesting that today we find many people teaching in our churches who are not "apt" to teach; who do not have the aptitude or ability to get the job done adequately. On the one hand there are those who have the responsibility but not the capability. On the other hand there are those who have the ability but are overlooked or refuse to be of service. We must, with the help of God, adequately prepare ourselves for our ministry, and when we are prepared, we must engage in service to God and humanity. Whatever the call, *"give diligence to make your calling and election sure"* **(II Peter 1:10)**.

THE PATTERN

We must seek to find the form which our ministry will take based on the shape and pattern of previous ministries. We must not only seek divine guidance but we must also seek those who are gifted to lead others. We should pray for a spiritual director who can open our eyes as Ananias was able to open the eyes of Saul of Tarsus. **(Acts 9:10-18)**

Before we begin to devise new designs, we must study God's word and perceive the patterns from the past. Our pattern for ministry should take into consideration designs from the original patterns of history. We do not have to be locked into the patterns, but we should not discount them because they are from another era. We do not have to continue to re-invent the wheel.

Finally, our plan and design for service must be procedural. We must begin at the beginning and follow our course to the end. We must work out our plan step-by-step as we would follow a road map. We can not start out in the middle and expect to arrive at the appropriate place.

Our design must have a strategy and a scheme; a specific way of working to accomplish our task. We must develop a method of doing things. When we fail to plan, we plan to fail. Abraham was able to go out, not knowing where he was going **(Hebrews 11:8)** because he was being led by God, and he was following God's plan. We, on the other hand, must be very sure that we are being led by God or we will be wandering aimlessly in our ministry and our mission will only lead to frustration.

THE DIMENSIONS OF MINISTRY:

In our design of ministry, we must not only understand the biblical concept of the plan, the direction which our ministry will take, but we must also understand the dimensions of our ministry. We need a diagram for working out our ministry. Jesus gives us the "cross" as a working diagram to follow. He tells us to take up our cross. This could mean that we must develop a plan which incorporates the horizontal and the vertical dimensions. There are times when we must develop the ability to synthesize the ways of God with our best thoughts and with the wisdom of the ages.

God has not only spoken through great men and women in the past. He also has spoken to great people who have written these thoughts down for our edification. We must learn how to learn from others. As stated above, there are more important things for us to do in our day than to continually "re-invent the wheel." We must learn how and where to recognize truth and allow that truth to inform our actions. In speaking to the Christians in Corinth, Paul says that the events recorded in the Old Testament *"happened unto them for examples: and they are written for our admonition"* **(I Corinthians 10:11).**

In Saint Paul's prayer to God for the Christians at Ephesus, his desire for them was that they *"may be able to comprehend with all saints what is the breadth, and length, and depth, and height; and to know the love of Christ, which passeth knowledge, that ye might be filled with all the fullness of God"* **(Ephesians 3:18-19)**.

We must know, we must comprehend, the breadth of our ministry. Often we think that God's will and work is narrow, denominational, and exclusive. We must come to realize that although we may only have a small part in the ministry, God's design is universal. He told His first disciples that they were only to start in Jerusalem, but the breadth of their ministry was to be ever expanding to include Judea, and Samaria, and finally they were to reach to the utmost parts of the earth. **(Acts 1:8)**

Next, we must comprehend the length of our ministry. We are called to work until Christ returns for His Church. Our call and our duty is that *"this gospel of the kingdom shall be preached in all the world for a witness unto all nations; and then shall the end come"* **(Matthew 24:14)**.

And then again, we must comprehend the depth of our ministry. Often Christian service is shallow and insipid. We fail to give true substance to our ministry. Through lack of study, of commitment and dedication, and through lack of purpose and planning the mission and ministry suffer and often die. We must seek to ever deepen our desire and determination to do the work assigned to us, and to magnify and multiply the ministry of the Master. We must make FULL proof of our ministry. **(II Timothy 4:5)**

And lastly, the Christian saint and servant must comprehend the height of service. Although our work is on earth, it has heavenly ramifications. There is a partnership between ourselves and the risen, ascended Lord. We are His co-workers. We must understand that Christ is the Commander-in-chief and that we are responsible to Him and will someday be called upon to give an account to Him. We are not our own "boss" nor is any church or religious organization the final authority or judge of our work. Paul says that He that judges us is the Lord. **(I Corinthians 4:4)**

We must never lose sight of this eternal design of God. *"Where there is no vision, the people perish: but he that keepeth the law, happy is he"* **(Proverbs 29:18)**. The Apostle Peter stated that *"It shall come to pass in the last days, saith God, I will pour out of My Spirit upon all flesh: and your sons and your daughters shall prophesy, and your young men shall see visions, and your old men shall dream dreams: and on My servants and on My handmaids I will pour out in those days of My Spirit, and they shall prophesy"* **(Acts 2:17-18)**.

Therefore, we must not be afraid to dream big dreams. God has promised to give us visions and dreams, but with all of our hopes, and dreams, and visions, and desires, and aspirations, we must also follow the law of purposeful planning. Our way must coincide with God's way and our will must be to do His will. Any self-determined will or way shall fail. In our personal "garden of Gethsemane" we must seek God's will and submit our will to His. As Jacob wrestled with the angel of the Lord until he was in accord with God's will for his life, we too must be willing to strive to determine God's desire and design for our ministry.

CHAPTER 7

THE DEVELOPMENT OF THE MINISTRY

Both in the life of the Church and in the life of the individual there must be a continuous effort to discover and develop ministers and areas of ministry. The Church is a service organization and a serving organism. There must be continued growth and development or the entity will wane and die. No church or individual can settle for being lukewarm. God's people must be filled with a burning desire to serve and a growing ability to fulfill the responsibility of service.

Below is a list of areas where ministries and ministers must grow and develop. After designing the structure of the church and determining the guidelines for growth, it will be necessary to develop a "state-of-the-art" program which will, with the help of God, accomplish the desired goals of ministry. Training will be necessary for new people entering into tasks which they have not performed in the past, and re-training will be necessary for those who will need to do "old" tasks in "new" and "creative" ways.

Goals will have to be set in order to determine when a person is equipped to begin to provide service. There are serious dangers in sending out a person on a mission of ministry who is not prepared to achieve the desired goal.

Ephesians 4:11-15 says that there must be, *"the perfecting (equipping) of the saints, for the work of the ministry, for the edifying of the body of Christ: Till we all come in the unity of the faith, and of the knowledge of the Son of God, unto a perfect man, unto the measure of the stature of the fullness of Christ: That we henceforth be no more children, tossed to and fro, and carried about with every wind of doctrine, by the sleight of men, and cunning craftiness, whereby they lie in wait to deceive; But speaking the truth in love, may grow up into Him in all things, which is the head, even Christ..."*

The church has an equipping ministry. It must encourage and enable every member to learn and grow within the congregation. On a horizontal level, A church is no stronger than its members, and on the same level, a member is no stronger than he has been equipped to be by those who have this responsibility in the church.

1. First the Church and the Christian must have a developing purpose. There is an a priori need to understand the call to service before one can begin to grow and develop in that service. After the purpose has been determined there must be growth in the area of the purpose. The ministry must progressively expand in realizing why God has extended the call in general, and also the minister must realize why God has extended the call to him or her specifically. God is a personal, intimate deity, and He does not generalize in His will for us. God knows each of us personally and He addresses us and calls each of us by our name.

   God has a specific and special task and ministry for each of us. Many are called. God calls as surely and as clearly today as He called others down through biblical times. The demands of our times are no less serious than they were in the beginning of human history, and God's desire to work in and through us in a given situation is no less present today than it has been in the past.

   Today our churches must develop high aims and set large, as well as meaningful goals. During the gospel days, when Christ would call out His disciples, He would often take them up into a high mountain. The concept here is that He was always trying to raise and expand their horizons. So often we are not able to "see the forest for the trees."

   We settle for the small and the insignificant ministry rather than elevating our thinking to new heights. We must continue to strive deeper and higher for the fullness of our purpose in serving God and humanity. **Ephesians 3:18** tells us that we must *"be able to comprehend with all saints what is the breadth, and length, and depth, and height; and to know the love of Christ, which passes knowledge."* In order for us to acquire this level of knowledge, we must be disciples who are willing to follow Christ to higher heights of development.

   Through prayer, through meditation, through dialogue, through

Bible study, through worship, and through quiet times the purpose of our calling begins to grow clearer. Also His purpose begins to grow as we allow Him to work our His purposeful will in our lives.

2. We must also develop a rationale for the service we render. We are called to be awake and aware in our ministry. Jesus told His first disciples, and He tells His present day saints in **John 15:15**, *"Henceforth I call you not servants; for the servant knoweth not what his lord doeth: but I have called you friends; for all things that I have heard of My Father I have made known unto you."* Although what we do in the service to God and mankind makes us "servants," who we are in our partnership, relationship and fellowship to Christ makes us His "friends."

   Our work for God is not a meaningless, mindless work. God does not engage us in "busy" work, but for everything that He assigns, He also has a reason. There are underlying principles for our work on earth. We must not only seek to have a better understand of what we are doing but we must also understand why we are doing the task. We can discover the "what" of things by digging deeper. We can only understand the "why" of life by allowing God to reveal this by His Holy Spirit.

   God has His own timetable and in His own time He will reveal things to us. To discover and develop our purpose for service is up to each of us. To discover and develop the rationale for our service is mostly up to God. It has been said that we must work as though everything depends on us, and, we must pray as though everything depends on God.

   Although our ministry may at sometimes appear strange and mysterious to us and to others, it is always logical and rational from God's perspective. We must become increasingly more adept in seeing things God's way and strive to develop a divine viewpoint regarding our ministry. If we are patient, God will progressively reveal His will and His way to His ministers. God will not only give us responsibilities but He will also give us reasons with the responsibilities. To have a developing ministry, we must have a God-given vision. Where there is no vision, the people not only perish (**Proverbs 29:18**), but they first an foremost fail to develop or thrive.

3. Those who have a mission of ministry must develop a growing understanding of the policies which determine their action. Once we understand the reason for our ministry we must also understand the fact that we must be reasonable in the way we work out our ministry.

   Philippians 2:12-13 warns us to *"Work out your own salvation with fear and trembling. For it is God which worketh in you both to will and to do of His good pleasure."* The Apostle Paul is saying that ministry is serious business. We must realize that God is the Great Lawgiver. He is the Designer of the universe. We can not have things our way, but we must do things God's way. God rules and super-rules in the affairs of Humanity.

   We must seek to know, interpret and comprehend the rules which govern our divine service. We might know sociology, psychology and philosophy, but we must not use these to determine what is right or wrong regarding our life's work. It is God who calls, and it is God who guides us in the way He would have us go in our work. We not only have a policy as a guiding principle, but we also have an "insurance" policy which assures us that if we do things according to God's will, we are certified to be rewarded according to God's word.

4. Next we must develop a proposal for service. We must take the time and write out what we will do and how we will do it.

   As earlier stated, we must be creative in our ministry, we should have ideas and suggestions of new and innovative ways to meet the needs and demands of our day. We should be like Abraham who proposed a way by which Sodom might be saved **(Genesis 18)**. God wants us to seek to save those who are lost, and if we can propose ways which are contemporary but are anchored in biblical principles, God can weave these proposals into His plan.

5. As God has an eternal plan for His creation, we too are called to develop our ability to be planners. We must plan our work and then we must work our plan. We must have a "blue print" for our ministry. As we grow and develop in our ministry, we should also grow in being able to dream kingdom dreams and work out earthly plans. We are not to follow the plans of the world but we should be as wise as the children of this world in being able to plan. We are not called to be business men and women but we should conduct our affairs in a business-like way. We are called to be "harmless as doves," but we are also called to be "wise as serpents" **(Matthew 10:16)**.

6. Our developed plans should flow into a developed and developing program. Our program should be systematic, consistent and cohesive. There must be an organized, systematized (yet spiritual) way of doing ministry. We should know what the Program of the church is, and we should make known the Program of the church to those both within the congregation and those within the community. We should never confuse the "programs" of the church with the "Program" of the Church. God's Program supersedes our programmatic activities.

   There are many things which we do in our churches today, but we must never forget why the Church exists. The Church has a God given mission of ministry and if that is forgotten, the church fails to be the true Church of Christ. We must continually evaluate the work of the church and our individual service in and through the Church. If we find that we are off course, we must revise our program or any components as needed.

7. It was stated earlier that God is a God of Order. We too must develop order in our Christian work. Jesus gives us the process and procedure of growth and development in **Mark 4:28** where He says growth entails *"first the blade, then the ear, after that the full corn in the ear."* Things must work out according to procedure, and we must devise ways of following a pattern or map in the working out of our ministry.

   We must learn to put first things first in all that we do. We must learn to set priorities in our ministry. We can not do a thing first because it is easy or because it will make us popular. We must follow God's way, and to do this, we must have open communication with God. We must pray before we begin our work; we must pray while we work; and we must pray at the conclusion of our work, as we commend our work into the hand of God. Then the Church, as she is led by The Holy Spirit, can develop a procedure that is in keeping with the will of God.

8. An exciting aspect of developing a sense of ministry is to develop special projects which will give growth to the Church and glory to God. The Church should come together to "brain-storm" to find new and significant ways to minister. There is always more than one way to do something, and there is also more than one mission and ministry which we can attempt for God. So often we get locked into doing mission and ministry in the same old way, or we believe that there are no new and meaningful missions or ministries open to the Church today. New times present the opportunity to do new things in radically new ways. We can discover and develop new projects which have never been thought of or tried before.

9. This also leads to strategies old and new. We need to learn how to do strategic planning. In **Matthew 10:16** Jesus says, *"Behold, I send you forth as sheep in the midst of wolves; be ye therefore wise as serpents, and harmless as doves."* We must have a good scheme for carrying out our plans. Often *"the children of this world are in their generation wiser than the children of light."*

(Luke 16:8) The Church and the individual Christian can not be formidable opponents against the forces of evil if there is no developing desire and ability to use appropriate strategy.

10. The minister must discover, design and develop tools to be used in the service to God and humanity. Moses had a rod, Aaron also had a rod, David had a sling shot. Paul said in **Ephesians 6:11** that we are to put on the whole armor of God. Scripture tells us that Jesus was a carpenter **(Matthew 13:55 and Mark 6:3)**. This tells us that He both had tools and was proficient in the use of them.

    We can not go out empty-handed into our ministry. We must know how to use our Bible, our hymn book, our commentaries, etc. These are some of our tools. Then we have the pen, and the typewriter or computer, the internet, the television, the radio, the automobile, the public address system, which also serve us in our service to others. Human beings became civilized when they developed an understanding of how to make tools and how to use them to accomplish their tasks. Our ministries will advance as we become proficient in the use of all of the tools and equipment available to us to assist us to be successful in our ministry.

11. Jesus was amazing in the way He healed the sick. Often He would vary His technique in performing a miracle. In healing the lepers and in healing the blind, He used different means at different times. We too should develop the ability to vary our technique in our Christian service. We need to learn to share with each other and teach each other different ways of accomplishing the same task. Often one approach might turn a person off while another approach will win them to Christ. We should not become locked into one procedure or one technique in performing our service. Maybe it is true that variety is the spice of life after all.

12. Finally we must develop the ability to function professionally, even within the church. The Christian worker must be fully trained and prepared for the work to which he/she has been called and selected.

The Apostle Peter says in **II Peter 1:10** that we are to *"give diligence to make your calling and election sure..."* We can no longer settle for mediocrity in God's Church among God's People. We are to make every effort to fulfill the god-given assignment with enthusiasm and zeal. The Church must both encourage and require it's leaders to be equipped for service.

The Church can also develop professionally by developing a ministerial staff not only in the preaching ministry, but in every aspect of Church life. No person in the Church should have a solo, or isolated ministry. When Jesus sent the disciples out, He sent them out two-by-two. **(Luke 10:1ff.)** We are called to labor together in the work of "Kingdom building." We are called not only to "work," but we are also called to "team-work."

We must develop a plan and procedure for team ministry. We must work to develop the individual into a staff, and develop the staff into a team, and the team into a congregation and the congregation into a Church, and then we must develop the Church into a single ministry which functions as the " Body of Christ." When we have accomplished this feat, then Christ, the Head of the Church can lead us out as one united army to win the world for Him.

CHAPTER 8

THE DISTINCTIONS OF THE MINISTRY

This may very well be one of the most important chapters in this book. It is also an important, and yet misunderstood dimension of Church life. **Ephesians 4:12** speaks of the "perfecting (equipping) the saints, for the work of ministry..." If we are not certain of the particular ministry for which one is to be equipped, then we run into confusion in accomplishing our task.

What the Apostle Paul states in **Romans 12:4-8** gives us a somber warning. He says, *"For as we have many members in one body, and all members have not the same office (function): So we, being many, are one body in Christ, and every one members one of another. Having then gifts differing according to the grace that is given to us, whether prophecy, let us prophesy according to the proportion of faith; Or ministry, let us wait on our ministry; or he that teacheth, on teaching; Or he that exhorteth, on exhortation: he that giveth, let him do it with simplicity; he that ruleth, with diligence; he that showeth mercy, with cheerfulness."*

Paul here is showing the variety, or distinctions, of ministries in the Church, that is, the body of Christ. We often fail, as did that first century Church, to realize that God has given to each person in the Church a duty or ministry to preform. **II Peter 1:10** warns us that we are to *"give diligence to make our calling and election sure."* **II Timothy 4:5** tells us to *"make full proof of your ministry."*

Over the years we have arrived at a place where the word and title "minister" has become synonymous with the words and titles "preacher" and "pastor." We have greatly limited the understanding of the early church and consequently we have limited the breadth of ministerial functions which could happen in the church and through the church into the world. There are those who desire to be involved and to serve in the church. They do not feel, however, that they have been called to the "preaching" ministry. Sometimes they are convinced against their will to preach anyway. Sometimes they change their thinking and feeling, and go into the "preaching" ministry. At other times they become frustrated and do not serve at all.

In this chapter we look at Christian ministries from "A" to "Z." This list and discussion does not exhaust the possibilities of service in and through the church. This chapter only begins to expand our concept of "ministry" and begin to broaden, widen, lengthen, deepen, and heighten our vistas and the latent potential within the church.

Each church can discover, design and develop a broad range of ministers and ministries with their congregation through developing a program of assessing the demands in the community and then surveying those with a deep desire to be used to the glory of God. With this in mind we search the alphabets, and we begin to search our churches for ministers.

AMBASSADORS: The Apostle Paul says on several occasions that a major role of ministry is that of "ambassador". In **I Corinthians 5:20** he says, *"Now then we are ambassadors for Christ, as though God did beseech you by us; we pray you in Christ's stead, be ye reconciled to God."* In **Ephesians 6:19-20** he states, *"And (pray) for me, that utterance may be given unto me, that I may open my mouth boldly, to make known the mystery of the gospel, For which I am an ambassador in bonds; that therein I may speak boldly, as I ought to speak."*

Paul had a clear understanding of the position he had in the body of Christ and the duty he was expected to play in representing his Savior in the world of his day. Paul also calls the Christian to understand and fulfill the task of ambassador.

We have a ministry not only in the church and to the church, but also a ministry between the world and the Creator. God has ordained that those who become "new" creatures must work with Him to bring about a "new" creation. God, the divine sovereign of the universe, has chosen those whom He calls to be ambassadors and to be reconcilers for Him.

It is interesting that this starts out the list of distinctive ministries. It is one of the most crucial, and yet it might be one of the least recognized. Many of our problems which exist in our society are due to a break-down in relationships. There is alienation between races, sexes, cultures, religions, and nations. Ultimately we as humans are alienated from God. The demand of our time, as it has been historically, is for reconciliation and solidarity. It was Christ's prayer that God might make us one. **(John 17:11, 21-23)**

The will of God is that there will be those who will enter into the ministry of reconciliation and become ambassadors for Christ. In nations an ambassador is a diplomatic official of highest rank who has been appointed or chosen to represent his government while living in another country or territory. An "ambassador" for Christ is one who lives in the world and yet is a representative of highest rank for heaven.

If we are to change the divisions, the estrangement, the alienation which exists in our world today, we must be able to discover and develop a cadre of ambassadors who can stand between the sacred and the secular, between the church and the market-place, between heaven and earth, and allow God to work in them to bring us to a place of "oneness."

BRANCHES OF THE VINE: In **John 15:1-6** Jesus says, *"I am the vine, and My Father is the husbandman. Every branch in Me that beareth not fruit He taketh away: and every branch that beareth fruit, He purgeth it, that it may bring forth more fruit. Now ye are clean through the word which I have spoken unto you. Abide in Me, and I in you. As the branch cannot bear fruit of itself, except it abide in the vine; no more can ye, except ye abide in Me. I am the vine, ye are the branches: He that abideth in Me, and I in him, the same bringeth forth much fruit: for without Me ye can do nothing. If a man abide not in Me, he is cast forth as a branch, and is withered; and men gather them, and cast them into the fire, and they are burned."*

This ministry and metaphor speaks of our worship and work as members of the church, which is the body of Christ. We are as much a part of Christ as a branch is a part of a vine. The same life force which flows through the vine flows through the branches. The same one who cares for the vine cares for the branches. The relationship between the vine and the branches is reciprocal, and yet the vine can exist without the branches, however, the branches cannot exist without the vine.

Those who are called to abide in Christ are called to a very special and sacred place in the body. This is the church within the church. This is the inner circle. This was the place of Peter, James and John. They had a close and abiding place and relationship with Christ. During Christ's earthly ministry, these three were seldom seen apart from Him. Christ nurtured these three disciples and gave them special opportunities for service.

Those who are close to Christ are those who produce special fruit. It is incumbent upon each church in every generation to seek out those among the congregation who are as "fruit-bearing branches." This is a special God-given ability which all ministries do not have. **Psalm 1:3** declares *"And he shall be like a tree planted by the rivers of water, that bringeth forth his fruit in his season; his leaf also shall not wither; and whatsoever he doeth shall prosper."* **Hebrews 11th** chapter lists many of these people who have historically filled this ministry and provided this service. There are those even today who are "branches."

As the branch cannot exist without the Vine, the church cannot exist without fruit-bearers. A major priority of each church must be to allow those who can bear fruit to do so. This ties in with personal evangelism, where a "fruit-bearer" can often win more souls for Christ than a week of revival services are able to do with the help of a congregation, choirs, and a special guest preacher.

The "fruit-bearer" can produce more disciples alone than a professional group can do together. And a "fruit-bearer" can bring a church closer to its place in God's Program than all of the planning programs and committees can accomplish.

CHOSEN RACE: **I Peter 2:9** says that God's people are very special. The first of his distinctions is that God's people are a "chosen race." This is not a "badge of distinction" but rather it entails a distinctive call to responsibility to God's world and an accountability to God's will. The Apostle Peter says we are chosen to *"shew forth the praises of Him who hath called you out of darkness into marvelous light."*

Matthew 5:16 says, *"Let your light so shine before men, that they may see your good works, and glorify your Father which is in heaven."* As the lamp-lighter of olden times had a special job and as the Olympic runner also had a task of providing light, so the Christian Church has a general purpose to provide light in a dark world.

Those persons who are chosen as "lamp-lighters" address the need for light in various ways. The world is in intellectual darkness, and there are those who write and teach on Christian values and seek to inculcate ethical principles and biblical doctrine. Our present age is incumbered with individuals with dark desires, and those who are called out of the "chosen generation" are servants of morality and ministers of purity of heart.

God's Word says that *"few are chosen"* **(Matthew 22:14)**. This being the case, we must seek to discover who and where this remnant of individuals are, and we must deploy them in service to the glory of God. As Christ's life can flow into His servants as the life flows from the vine to the branch, so too can His light flow from Himself to those who are the lights of the world, the "chosen generation."

DISCIPLES: When Jesus calls men and women into discipleship, it is a call not only to become His students and study in His word and His way. His call is also for us to become ministers and to serve in His work and according to His will.

There is so much talk about discipleship, and so much has been written about the subject. What is really needed is for us to do the ministry rather that to speak and study about the work of the disciple. To be a disciple or follower of Christ is to engage in ministry as He did during his sojourn on earth.

Luke 9:23 says, *"If any man will come after me, let him deny himself, and take up his cross daily, and follow me."* This Scripture points out that there is a process which leads to this service of discipleship. The first phase is self-denial. Before we can serve as a disciple, we must be willing, ready, and able to deny ourselves. We cannot concentrate on Christ or the needs of others if our thoughts are centered on ourselves and our needs. We must learn how to set priorities by leaving our concerns in God's hands so that our hands can be free to do the work of Christ.

The work which we have to do is summed up in the term "cross-bearing." It is impossible to pick up a cross if our hands are filled with our cares and our problems. It is amazing how our burdens become lessened when we shoulder up the burdens of another. Then Jesus not only tells us to take up our cross, but Luke tells us that we are to do this "daily." This is the second phase of this crucial ministry. We must bear the crosses of others because there is no profession or occupation in secular society which can fill the need in our society for cross-bearing. If the Christian does not bear the crosses of others, it will not get done. The final phase is that we follow Christ with cross in hand.

This mission of ministry is without a doubt the area where the largest number of servants are needed. There are people, places and times in our society when it will take more than one individual to carry a cross. There will be times when there will be the need for a team to carry a cross. There are times when disciples will have to go out two-by-two and three-by-three in order to be effective in service. Crosses get heavy and cumbersome and without joint ministry, the job often cannot be done.

If there is a ministry which will take continued discovery, development and deployment, this aspect of discipleship is one of those areas. The good news and the difficult news is that the Christian Church can "make" disciples, which means that a continuous supply of individuals are available, but we must exercise every effort to groom these individuals into the personalities and servants who can then deny themselves, take up their cross, and follow Christ.

This is commanded of us by Christ. In **Matthew 20:19**. The promise given is that Christ Himself will be present to assist and support in this important task of disciple-making. Given the great lack of disciples and the great need for disciples, it is encouraging to know than we can duplicate disciples in the life of the church. Now we must make this a high priority in the life of every congregation.

ELECT: **Romans 8:33a** states, *"Who shall lay anything to the charge of God's elect?* This Scripture and others which deal with the subject of the "elect" imply that there is something very special about this office. These are those who are especially selected by God Himself. These persons are not appointed by a pastor, nor are they recommended by a search committee, nor are they voted on by a congregation. The elect are God's "elect" and are chosen by God.

The elect have a sacred post as well as a special place in God's economy and in God's Church. **Matthew 24:22-31** and **Mark 13:20-27** both tell us that because of the elect, God will determine the time of the end, and the elect will be gathered from throughout the world before the final destruction.

The elect are similar to Abraham's nephew Lot who stayed the hand of God's wrath until he was safely out of Sodom (**Genesis 19**). This was also true regarding the life of Methuselah. Because of Enoch, who walked with God, the flood did not come nor did God destroy the world until Enoch's son, Methuselah died.

Those "elect" who are put in special places at special times may not always be aware of their ministry but yet who they are and what they do is as effective as the greatest revivalist, or the greatest evangelist, or the greatest prophet.

The church must seek to discern and distinguish those whom God has selected and elected. Through prayer, it is possible to see at least through a "glass darkly" what God is doing in His church and in His world. In **II Kings 6:17** *"the (Prophet) Elisha prayed"*, when he and his servant were surrounded by the enemy, *"and said, Lord, I pray thee, open his eyes, that he may see. And the Lord opened the eyes of the young man; and he saw: and, behold, the mountain was full of horses and chariots of fire round about Elisha."* God has His special servants, and His special servants have special protection from God, so that they might be able to accomplish their tasks.

FAITHFUL: **Matthew 25:21, 23** says, *"His lord said unto him, Well done, thou good and faithful servant: thou hast been faithful over a few things, I will make you ruler over many things: enter thou into the joy of thy lord."* This parable tells of those servants whose service, or responsibility, is to be faithful. A very crucial ministry in every age is for men and women who can say with Martin Luther: "Here I stand, God being my help, I cannot recant," or who can say with the Apostle Paul - in **Ephesians 6:13**, *"...and having done all, to stand."* The Scriptures say that the just shall live by their faithfulness (**Habakkuk 2:4** and **Romans 1:17**).

The great service these ministers of faith render in the church and in the world is the teaching by example of the trusting relationship which a true child should have with the Father. This is a very difficult task because often one must be faithful when conditions are not favorable. The Old Testament prophets were called by God and expected to be faithful when even their own family and friends turned against them.

There is an increasing need today for those who are able to keep the faith and keep faithful in what is being called a "post-Christian" age. The faithful ministry is not a popular one. Often there is ridicule and sometimes even those in the church become adverse to the stand taken by the faithful servant, or the person who serves by the task of faithfulness.

One of the great services which can be performed today is to take a stand against injustice in local, state and federal government. There is a need for men and women to stand up against the breakdown of moral and ethical values. **Jeremiah 5:1** says *"Run ye to and fro through the streets of Jerusalem, and see now, and know, and seek in the broad places thereof, if ye can find a man, if there be any that executeth judgment, that seeketh truth: and I will pardon it."* Even in our day there is the same need for "faithful" men and women.

GODLY: **Titus 2:11-12** tells us, *"For the grace of God that bringeth salvation hath appeared to all men, Teaching us that, denying ungodliness and worldly lusts, we should live soberly, righteously, and godly, in this present world."* The message here is that God needs many servants who are willing to live pious, devout lives in the midst of the ungodliness which we see all around us. People learn by imitation and example, and there is the need for Christian men and women in the "market-place" to reflect the nature of God. We are made in God's image and likeness, and we must be examples of His character as we go about our daily activities.

This is another example of Christians letting their light shine in the world. Our presence in society should be illuminating to those who find themselves in moral and spiritual darkness. For many people outside of the church, the godly servant is the only representation of the divine which they will ever see. This is such a crucial ministry. It does not take a lot of talking or preaching. It only takes a willingness to stand in the "midst." The world is watching the church and its members. Often when a worldly person sees a Christian living godly, it challenges them to seek a more perfect life.

When the Godly person can be a source of peace in times and places of trouble, they show the message of Jesus in **Matthew 5:9**, that says, *"Blessed are the peacemakers: for they shall be called the children of God."* So often in the church and in the world the person and minister who is missing in church meetings and secular board meetings is that godly person who can make peace when others are making war.

The task of the churches is to identify those persons who have this special grace of godliness. We must continue to discover these people in our congregation and then we must deploy them in the church and in the society to be used to the glory of God.

HOLY NATION: As we stated earlier, Peter says in his first letter that *"Ye are a chosen generation, a royal priesthood, an holy nation..."* This writing points out another ministry of the Christian Church. We are not only called to ministry, but we are also called to group or team ministry. We are called to join together as the people of God. We are called and chosen to be a mighty nation of people.

It has been the Satan's plot to drive wedges between us and attempt to make us serve in isolation. He realizes that when he divides us it is easy to conquer us. Jesus showed us this need for team ministry when he immediately began to call followers at the very beginning of His earthly ministry. **Mark 3:14** says, *"And He ordained twelve, that they should be with Him, and that He might send them forth to preach."* Before Jesus commissioned His disciples, he chose them to "be" with Him. This team ministry approach created an opportunity for relationship and partnership.

We too are called to be in ministry with Christ and with one another. We are one nation and that nation is a holy nation. Everyone in the nation is not holy, even as every one in this nation is not an American, but we are all joined together. Jesus says that the wheat and the tares will grow together. **(Matthew 13:25-30)**

When we pray that God's kingdom will be established on earth as it is in heaven, **(Matthew 6:10)** we are also showing the presence of that kingdom and the fulfillment of that prayer when we are able to live and function together as a "holy nation." Each individual in the church should strive to serve in this capacity. It is possible to fill a number of these distinct ministries in the body. This one should be a requirement for every member.

INTERCESSORS: In **I Timothy 2:1** Paul says, *"I exhort therefore, that, first of all, supplications, prayers, intercessions, and giving of thanks, be made for all men."* Paul's instructions to Timothy and to us today is that we have a ministry and a responsibility to pray for "everybody." The church is not only committed to pray for other Christians, but the church must pray for the world.

The call to pray is a call to intercede to God on the behalf of others. **Acts 12:5** says, **"Peter therefore was kept in prison: but prayer was made without ceasing of the church unto God for him." II Chronicles 6th** chapter gives the beautiful intercessory prayer of King Solomon for all people and **II Chronicles 7th** chapter gives God's answer and promise to King Solomon's prayer. God said to the King and to us that **(II Chronicles 7:14)** *"If My people, which are called by My name, shall humble themselves, and pray, and seek My face, and turn from their wicked ways; then will I hear from heaven, and will forgive their sin, and will heal their land."*

This is one of the greatest promises of the Scriptures and it is a response to the service of intercession. If a preacher has a team of intercessors, he will find great power to proclaim the gospel. If an Evangelist is supported by "prayer warriors" who fulfill this ministry of intercession, there will be many souls who will accept Christ. If missionaries are sustained in their mission work by those who have this distinct ministry, there will be a great spread of the gospel throughout all the world.

The church must seek out men and women who are willing to pray for situations which confront us today. Our youth and elderly, our local and national leaders need intercessory prayer. We must not only pray for our own, but we must pray for all people. As long as there are churches which continue to meet weekly for prayer, no matter how small the gathering, there will be blessed promises fulfilled by God. Jesus said that if there are only two persons who meet together for intercessory prayer, He will be in the midst **(Matthew 18:19-20)**.

JUSTIFIED: **Romans 8:28-30** tells us that *"We know that all things work together for good to them that love God, to them who are the called according to His purpose....Moreover whom He did predestinate, them He also called: and whom He called, them He also justified: and whom He justified, them He also glorified."* The good news of this scripture is that because God is at work in all things and God is at work in our lives, we are made just before Him.

In the ministry of the "just" there is the living example of the goodness, mercy and grace of God. The just are an expression of God's love for each generation. Those who are in the world as a living presence of God's salvation serve to lead others to salvation. Someone has said that Christianity is not only "taught" but it is also "caught." Those who have been called and justified are also sent into the world to show and tell of the grace of God.

There are many today who are making every attempt to be accepted, to gain approval. When they encounter those who are able to show what God has done in their life, there is a kind of contagion of faith which will cause a lost soul to seek to emulate that justified servant.

KEEPERS: **Genesis 4:9** says, *"And the Lord said unto Cain, Where Is Abel thy brother? And he said, I know not: Am I my brother's keeper?"* This is the first murder recorded in the Scriptures. More than that, this is the first total denial of one's responsibility for another. Abel was one who had some sense of responsibility. Verse two says that Abel was a *"keeper of sheep."* It seems that some of the greatest leaders in the Bible were *"keepers of sheep"*. Jesus called Himself the Good Shepherd **(John 10:14)**, and King David called God his Shepherd **(Psalm 23:1)**.

There is the need today for men and women to know what it takes to tend to others. There are so many persons both young and old who need to experience the "keeper" ministry. Jesus told Peter in **John 21:15-17** to be a keeper of His sheep. This is a ministry of love. Cain was not his brother's keeper because his heart was filled with jealousy and hatred. We can only truly care for those whom we love. The shepherd ministry is one of loving care for others.

To be a keeper is to care not only for people but to also care for things. A janitor is a kind of "keeper." He/she is responsible for keeping the building and grounds in good shape. When the grass needs to be cut and the hedges trimmed, there must also be a desire to see God's property neat and clean. Those who work in nursing homes and orphanages and hospitals are also keepers. Sometimes we are not able to help to promote health and wholeness, but we can have a "keeping" ministry. We can help a brother or sister to keep the faith, to hope in God and to keep holding on to God's unchanging hand.

Those who perform this ministry must be willing to sacrifice for the other. To be a keeper means that one must be willing to give of their time, of their energy, of their resources, and of their place in society for the other person. It means to be willing to surrender all.

LIGHT: **Matthew 5:14**, *"Ye are the light of the world. A city set on a hill cannot be hid. Neither do men light a candle, and put it under a bushel, but on a candlestick; and it giveth light unto all that are in the house. Let your light so shine before men, that they may see your good works, and glorify your Father which is in heaven."*

This is one of the most significant ministries specified by our Savior. When He speaks to His followers about being the "Light of the world," He is calling them to be a source of inspiration and illumination both within the church (giving light to all that are in the house) and in the world (shining before men).

There are four major areas of responsibility for those called to be a "Light." First there are those who "show" or illustrate through their living, personal examples of what it is like to have the Spirit of Christ, "The Light of the World," present in their lives. There are those who are able to live a radiant life in the church and in the "marketplace" which is a "show and tell" of the kind of life to which we have been called. All Christians are not able to "shine" in all situations. There are those in the church, however, who are blessed because they are able to rejoice when men revile and persecute them.

Second, the Christian is called to "shine" morally. In a world darkened by moral and ethical decline, the minister who is a "light" is one who can bring a presence of awareness of standards and values to a society which has lost proper guidelines for "right" living. There are those whose involvement in social, economic and political affairs causes those who have become jaded by drive for success to pause and reconsider their priorities. Those who have the light of Christ in their lives can reveal the shortcomings of others in a way that might lead to a change of heart and mind.

The third way in which a ministry of "light" shines in our world is as intellectual enlightenment. Our times have become dull and dark because of a lack of Christian teaching. The Christian can illuminate the minds of others by sharing the principles of the Faith. There are those who fail to comprehend the true meaning of life. Many today lack meaning, purpose and direction in life. There are those who are not able to properly chose and decide on the major concerns which confront us today. The Christian cannot hid his/her ability to caution and correct those who are going astray.

The last function of those who have the ministry of being a "light" in our world is on a spiritual level. The greatest task of any Christian is to provide a Christ-like presence wherever they are. The Apostle Paul was able to say, *"Christ liveth in me."* This being so, His Spirit also shines through me. If the world is in intellectual, moral, spiritual darkness today, it is because we are failing to provide the ministry of Light. Jesus says in **John 9:5** *"As long as I am in the world, I am the light of the world."* The Christian Church is responsible for keeping Christ present in every aspect of our social order.

MESSENGER: **Matthew 11:10,** *"This is he, of whom it is written, Behold, I send My messenger before Thy face, which shall prepare Thy way before Thee"* (Also found in **Mark 1:2**, and **Luke 7:27**). It is impossible to determine which of the many services rendered by God's ministers is greatest. Each has its importance in special times and conditions. This call to be a "messenger," however, is a very significant task. The above Scripture speaks of John the Baptist and his unique call by God to be the forerunner for Christ, the Messiah. In every age God has those whom He calls and sends to carry a word for their time.

God has always used a man or woman to be His spokesperson and to deliver His divine oracle. Although God has conveyed a message in a variety of ways over the pages of history, His most usual way has been to designate an individual to speak for Him. This is a dangerous task and yet it is a task of great distinction.

When God speaks to us, it is impossible to keep Him from speaking through us. **Jeremiah 20:9** reports, *"Then I said, I will not make mention of Him, nor speak anymore in His name. But His word was in my heart as a burning fire shut up in my bones, and I was weary with forebearing, and I could not stay."*

Amos 3:8-9 states that *"Surely the Lord will do nothing but He reveals His secret unto His servants the prophets. The lion hath roared, who will not fear? the Lord God hath spoken, who can but prophesy?"* Also we read the statement of Paul in **I Corinthians 9:16** which says, *"...necessity is laid upon me; yea, woe is unto me, if I preach not the gospel."* To be God's messenger is an urgent business, and to be used by Him is a blessed opportunity.

NURSE: **I Thessalonians 2:7**, *"But we were gentle among you, even as a nurse cherisheth her children."* Every type of service rendered in the body of Christ has a special purpose. The "nurse" has the responsibility of providing care under the supervision of the Great Physician, Jesus Christ.

There is the need for those who can show tender loving care (T.L.C.) to those who are not able to care for themselves. A healing and sustaining ministry is vital to the people of God. A church cannot function without being given nursing care from time to time.

Although the Apostle Paul was able to see himself as a strong soldier, he was also able to see himself as a tender nurse. We too must have both a firm and soft personality. There are times when we are called to fight, but there are times when we must bind up the wounds of others.

No Christian can claim to be filled with the Fruit of the Spirit without possessing the quality of gentleness. **Galatians 5:22-23** says that *"The fruit of the spirit is love, joy, peace, longsuffering, gentleness, goodness, faith, meekness, temperance: against such there is no law."* There are those who think that nursing is a "female" service, but truly this is a Christian ministry. When there is a need for T.L.C., there is no distinction between male or female. Love is a natural quality. The Good Samaritan in **Luke 10:30-37** epitomizes this "nursing" quality in the parable given by Jesus to the question, *"Who is my neighbor?"* My neighbor is that person who can depend on me when in need and that person upon whom I can depend when I am in need.

ORDAINED: **Romans 1:1,** *"Paul, a servant of Jesus Christ, called to be an apostle, separated (anointed, ordained, appointed, set apart) unto the gospel of God."* This service of the "ordained" is special in both the Old and the New Testament. Today, however it has been made to be ceremonial and elevated above the meaning in biblical days. Jesus reminded His Disciples that those who were "appointed" to positions of leadership were not to "lord" it over others; but those who were great were to be servants and those who were the greatest were to be servants of all **(Matthew 20:26-27)**.

To be ordained is to be "anointed" for sacred service. In the Old Testament days it was the kings, priests and prophets who were anointed. This signified that they were specially selected or appointed by God for holy service. There were special ingredients used and instructions given in the preparation of the anointing oil. This oil was to be used only for those who were appointed by God. These were the "elect."

And then to be ordained was to be "set apart." Paul was "set apart" for the ministry and in **Acts 13:2**, the Holy Spirit gave the instructions that Barnabas and Saul (Paul) be *"set apart"* for the work *"whereunto I have called them."* There are certain ministries or services in the church where the servant is *"set apart"* in the performing of his/her task. The preacher stands on an elevated platform or pulpit to convey this aspect of being *"set apart."*

Then there is the idea of ordination as being *"separated."* **Acts 13:48** says that *"As many as were ordained to eternal life believed."*

Matthew 25:32 says that Jesus *"shall separate them one from another."* This is a wider sense of the ordained which has to do with believers in general. There are those who are separated for specific tasks, and there are those who are separated for specific places.

Those who are OBEDIENT to God's word and His will are those who are ordained to do God's work. **Titus 3:1** says, *"Remind the people to obey the government and its officers, and always to be obedient and ready for any honest work."* The seven appointed in **Acts 6th chapter** were men of honest report who were filled with the Holy Spirit and wisdom. They were separated by the people and ordained to perform a special ministry.

PARTNERS: **Luke 5:10** speaks of James and John, sons of Zebedee, who were partners with Peter in their fishing business. A "partner" is an associate, colleague or ally who shares in a joint venture with others. In the Christian ministry, there is always the need for partnership. Both individual Christians and individual churches must work together to accomplish the ministry which has been given to the People of God. Even Jesus choose to work in partnership with His Disciples. **I Corinthians 10:17**, and other Scriptures remind us that we are "partakers" with Christ and with one another.

The Lord tells His followers in **Matthew 11:28** that we are to work in the "yoke" with Him. We are to be "yokefellows" as we labor together with our fellows in the service of the Lord.

This is one of the broad ministries of the church because of the added strength derived from joint effort. In pulling together, those who are strong can help to bear the infirmities of the weak (**Romans 15:1**). There is a certain comfort that we find in working together. Also when we are partners in unity, Jesus has promised to join with us (**Matthew 18:19-20**).

We are called to be as together as a "loaf" of bread. Paul says that we are one Loaf. When we become "bread" even as Jesus is Bread, our ministry will be to feed the hungry of the world. Jesus tells us to feed the hungry and we can fulfil this requirement when we, as Peter, James, and John are able to work together to be "fishers of men."

QUICK: This means that we are "alive." Jesus said that, *"I am come that they might have life, and that they might have it more abundantly."* **I John 3:16** states, *"Hereby perceive we the love of God, because He laid down His life for us: and we ought to lay down our lives for the brethren."* This is a hard saying. Jesus is saying that *"As He died to make us holy, we must be willing to make others free."* The call of Christ is a call for those who are alive, the "quick" to be willing to take up the cross daily and follow Him. We must be as willing as Paul to give up our life for the cause of Christ.

Most of Paul's letters speak of this need to make our bodies a living sacrifice **(Romans 12:1ff)**. When Christ returns, He will come for the "quick" and the dead **(Acts 10:42; I Peter 4:5)**. Christ is a Living Savior and He calls us to be a Living Church. We must be quick to hear **(James 1:19)** and quick to answer the call to service.

REDEEMED: **Isaiah 62:12** says, *"And they shall call them, The holy people, The redeemed of the Lord: and thou shalt be called, Sought out, a city not forsaken."* And in the New Testament, **Revelation 14:3-4** says, *"And they sung as it were a new song before the throne, and before the four beasts, and the elders: and no man could learn that song but the hundred and forty and four thousand, which were redeemed from the earth. These are they which were not defiled with women; for they are virgins. These are they which follow the Lamb withersoever He goeth. These were redeemed from among men, being the firstfruits unto God and to the Lamb."*

These two readings show us two pictures of the "redeemed." The first picture is that of the "redeemed" on earth. The second picture is that of the "redeemed" in heaven. This is a peculiar distinction which has eternal significance. These not only have a place and a purpose in time but also they have a place and a purpose in eternity.

These "redeemed" are people who have a holy nature. They are ministers of praise. They are those who rejoice and render praises to God. Also they are those who are praised by those who seek them out.

Matthew 5:16 tells us that when we let our light shine, people see our good works, and glorify God in heaven. This is how God's kingdom comes on earth as it is in heaven. A redeemed person is one in whose life the God of heaven reigns.

The "redeemed" do not wait to give praises to God in the next life. They do it both now and then. Their presence in the world is a spark of light and life in the midst of darkness and death. People of praise cause the promises of God to be fulfilled and the power and provisions of God to be made manifest. God often does great things for the sake of His people, the redeemed. When the redeemed of the Lord say "SO," then "SO" IT IS.

SALT: **Matthew 5:13**, *"Ye are the salt of the earth: but if the salt have lost his savor, wherewith shall it be salted? it is good for nothing, but to be cast out, and trodden under foot of men."* This distinctive service can be called the most practical and functional. This is stated in the first recorded sermon of Jesus. It is basic to His teaching and preaching. Jesus often told His disciples about their responsibility for service. Christian religion is more than ceremonies and personal growth. Our faith exists for the health and welfare of society.

First, Jesus tells His followers that we are responsible for the preservation of life. The church is in the world to provide for health and healing. The church is a "balm of Gilead," an answer to the ills and sickness of our time. In every age, there is a need for workers in communities to get involved and interact as salt interacts on meat for restoration and preservation.

Second, the church has a responsibility of putting moral and ethical "flavor" into its surrounds. Due to bad influences around us, society takes on bad taste. Fads and poor thinking tend to destroy the moral fabric of our age. The church can provide a "savory" state of affairs when it is available and able to introduce good values into dangerous ideologies. When the church, as "salt" can be incorporated into the plans for the welfare of humanity, there can be a synthesis which will lead to improvement of the situation.

When the Christian community loses those who can render this vital service of being "salt," the society no longer seeks out the church for answers or for help and healing. When we lose our salt, we become "good for nothing." It is imperative for each church to identify those persons within it's congregation and then devise a plan for joining them together with those with like ministry in other congregations. The "salt of the earth," as salt in a shaker, becomes more effective when there is solidarity, for in unity there is strength.

THANKFUL: **Colossians 3:15-17** says, *"Let the peace of God rule in your hearts, to the which also ye are called in one body; and be ye thankful. Let the word of Christ dwell in you richly in all wisdom; teaching and admonishing one another in psalms and hymns and spiritual songs, singing with grace in your hearts to the Lord. And whatsoever ye do in word or deed, do all in the name of the Lord Jesus, giving thanks to God and the Father by Him."*

This service is often called "worship service." On the one hand there is a separation between worship and service, and yet the greatest service we render is our worship, when it comes from a grateful and thankful heart. The Spirit of the Triune God in our hearts causes continuous praise. Our total life is a life of thanksgiving. Paul says in **I Thessalonians 5:18** that we are to, *"In everything give thanks: for this is the will of God in Christ Jesus concerning you."*

The greatest ministry is the ministry that is coupled with the "ministry of praise." Whatever our task, we can do it in a spirit and in an attitude of praise. Praise is becoming of God's people. There is a difference between praise and thanksgiving. To praise God is to recognize with joy who He is, and to thank God is to rejoice in the things that He does. But we cannot separate who He is from what He does.

God appreciates our thanks and praise because these are expressions of our being awake and aware of His presence in our lives and in our world. God really does not rely on our expressions of gratitude. He is good to us even when we are oblivious to His goodness or when we are not conscious of His blessings. When we awaken to the reality of His presence, His power, and His provisions, we then realize our relationship to Him. It is because of this reality and realization that we can say "Abba," Father.

UNLEAVENED BREAD: **I Corinthians 5:6-8** tells us, *"...Know ye not that a little leaven leaveneth the whole lump? Purge out therefore the old* *leaven, that ye may be a new lump, as ye are unleavened. For even Christ our passover is sacrificed for us: Therefore let us keep the feast, not with old leaven, neither with the leaven of malice and wickedness: but with the unleavened bread of sincerity and truth."*

The Christian servant is a model and a minister. The servant must work out his/her salvation while working for the salvation of others. Service and sanctification must work hand-in-hand. God works in us as He works through us. We can not wait until we are completely without sin before we can provide Christian service, but we must continue work to purge out the corruption in our lives. We are called to serve with "sincerity" and with "truth."

We must be sincere and true because even if others cannot detect the wrong in us, it will still effect them. The truth of the matter is that what you don't know can hurt you, and "one bad apple can spoil a whole bushel." A little leaven will leaven the whole loaf. We must be sincere and true both in the church and in the world.

This is another case where it is not only what we do but what we are that is important and necessary. We must continuously subject ourselves to self-examination and to be examined by God. We must have some form of spiritual direction to lead and guide us into the ways of holiness.

We must be "unleavened bread." As the Christian Church, we must be real. We cannot be mixed with the ways and will of God and also with the will and ways of the world.

VICTORIOUS: **I Corinthians 15:57** says, *"Thanks be to God, which giveth us the victory through our Lord Jesus Christ."* The Christian minister is a victorious servant and is also a servant of victory. In The Revelation, Jesus tells each of the seven churches of Asia, and they are messages to churches down through the ages, that there must be an overcoming or victory in and through our mission of ministry.

There is a serious need today for churches to realize the many areas of failure in our society and then to question where we go wrong or fall short in our responsibilities. **I Peter 4:17** tells us that *"The time is come that judgment must begin at the house of God: and if it first begin at us, what shall the end be of them that obey not the gospel of*

God?" The truth of the matter is that if we who are Christians must be judged, then it is time now for us to judge ourselves.

If God says that we are to "succeed" and be "victorious," then failure is unexplainable unless we admit that we are not following God's Program. There are those who criticize Gamaliel's words in **Acts 5:38**, and yet his words hold true. There he says to the Jewish Council that "If this counsel or this work be of men, it will come to naught: But if it be of God, ye cannot overthrow it." God's word assures us that we can achieve impossible tasks with His help, and He has promised that He will never fail us or forsake us **(Hebrews 13:5)**.

Even with limited resources or with limited ability, we can be victorious. Moses with only a shepherd's staff was able to lead the People of God out of the land of bondage. Many "store-front" churches have been able to accomplish what great cathedrals have not been able to do. Even today God is able to give the victory to those who are willing to totally commit and dedicate their life to Him and to His service. He promises us as He promised Moses that if we go, He will go with us.

WITNESSES: **Acts 1:8**, *"But ye shall receive power, after that the Holy Ghost is come upon you: and ye shall be My witnesses."* Those who have been with Christ and who have been filled with the Holy Spirit are called to bear witness to others of Christ's life, ministry, death, and resurrection. The only way the world will know of God's love for us and His Son's sacrifice for us is if we share the story far and near.

If there is a lack of Christian fervor today it is because the spirit of witnessing has lost its power to ignite a spark of love and desire in others. When we can be filled with the "tongues of fire" as the early "witnesses," we can cause a great revival even in our time.

A great awakening comes about when there is an outpouring of the Holy Spirit. There is an outpouring when there is first an in pouring into the lives of Christian men and women. Today there are churches that have a lot of emotion and excitement. There are churches that have great programs of entertainment. These programs, however, have no depth or heart desire which is in tune with the will of God.

True witnesses are willing to go anywhere at any time to testify to the saving power of Christ. The early followers of Christ have set the example of what a true witness is and what a true witness does. Those in the first century who were witnesses were thrown in prison, stoned, beaten, ostracized and put to death. Being a witness is not a glorious service, but God, Himself, has promised that those who have a ministry of witnessing will ultimately be glorified. The Risen Christ tells the church, *"Be thou faithful unto death, and I will give thee a crown of life."* **(Revelation 2:10)**

X_ _ _ _ _ _ _ _: "X" is a symbol for any unknown or unnamed factor, thing, or person. There are some functions and ministries which cannot be defined, described, or named but they serve very important functions in the body of Christ and in the world.

Paul says in **I Corinthians 2:9** that, *"Eye hath not seen, nor ear heard, neither have entered into the heart of man, the things which God hath prepared for them that love Him."* Paul implies here that God has wonderful things in store for those who Love Him and Love to be in His service. This does not mean that there are some far off, distant, blessings, but rather that we can be involved in exciting ways in His kingdom, which are mysterious and out of the realm of human understanding.

There are many tasks which are routine, traditional and which are understood by people within the church and in the world. There are some ministries which are unexplainable. God has no "job description" for some Spirit-directed tasks. The Evangelist, Philip, one of the Seven, was drafted into temporary service to carry the gospel to an Ethiopian eunuch in the Gaza Desert (**Acts 8th chapter**), and there are many who are pressed into service without forewarning or any type of ecclesiastic endorsement. God often moves in mysterious ways, His wonders to perform.

We must always be open to the breaking in of the Spirit of God. There are many calls to serve which have not been fully understood. God, even in this day, is performing "New Things." It is the churches task to be ever awake and alert to where God is at work, what He is doing, and who He is using in radical ways to fulfill His will.

Philosophers, social theorists, psychologists, and others cannot comprehend the ways of God, for He has *"hid these things from the wise and prudent, and hast revealed them unto babes"* **(Luke 10:21)**.

YOKEFELLOW: **Philippians 4:3**, *"And I entreat thee also, true yokefellow, help those women which laboured with me in the gospel, with Clement also, and with other my fellow labourers, whose names are in the book of life."*

We are called to be co-laborers with other ministers and render service in unison, to the glory of God. The Lord does not call us to be mavericks, or lone wolves, or to work solo. Jesus promises that when we are able to work together in twos and threes, He also will work with us **(Matthew 18:19-20)**. No part of the Body of Christ can operate without the rest of the body parts.

We have a fellowship. This means that we must be "in the same boat" together. Religion is more that a system of ceremonies and moral rules and regulations. Religion, to be true religion, must also be a relationship. We must be in relationship with Christ, and we must also be in relationship with each other. In recent years we have allowed denominationalism to divide and sub-divide our churches.

We as members of the church, the body of Christ, are yoked together with one another and we are yoked together with Christ. We share a mutual ministry, a mutual concern, and a mutual love relationship with the triune God. We are one family and we are of one blood. Satan's greatest scheme is to drive a wedge between us along racial, cultural, ethnic, economic lines. It is Christ's desire that we be one.

ZEALOUS: **Ecclesiastes 9:10** Says, *"Whatsoever thy hand findeth to do, do it with thy might; for there is no work, nor device, nor knowledge, nor wisdom, in the grave whither thou goest."* The Apostle Peter tells us that we are to be diligent to *"make our calling and election sure"* **(II Peter 1:10)**.

There must be a total willingness to serve in that which God has assigned us to do. It is a service in and of itself to be zealous in the service of God. Christ says in **Revelation 3:15, 19**, *"I know thy works,* *that thou art neither cold nor hot: I would thou wert cold or hot. As many as I love, I rebuke and chasten: be zealous therefore, and repent."*

The "last word" in the Christian vocabulary is the word "**ZEAL.**" We are called to be "on fire" for God. As we are called to be "salt" to purify the world, and we are called to be "Light" to illuminate the world, we are called to be "zealous" and ignite the world. God calls us to be enthusiastic and diligent, totally devoted to Him and to His will. We must have a fervor which causes others to experience the Spirit of God. The Christian Church began with "fire" from heaven, and if the Church is to continue, it will be because of men and women who have been touched and filled with that same Fire.

The word which best expresses the nature of the Christian worker is "enthusiasm", which comes from a Greek word meaning to be "in God," to be inspired by God, to be eager, and to be filled with joy and ecstasy. Jesus says that if we abide in Him, our joy will be full **(John 15:11)**. One of Christ's first Disciples was Simon, who was called the Zealot **(Luke 6:15)**, and Christ is looking and calling servants who will be "Zealots" in His continuing ministry.

CHAPTER 9

THE DIVERSITIES OF THE MINISTRY

ADMINISTRATOR: This is a most important task or function in the church, or in any institution. An administrator is one who has charge of the organizing of the church and also who is responsible for the affairs of the organization; he or she is the one who directs the program and the one who manages the people and/or the process of the organization.

One who administers must be able to provide leadership in a formal way. The task involves managing the affairs or concerns of others. This can be done by an individual administrator or it can be coordinated by a group of individuals. These are the ones who make up the executive branch of a government or institution; and the ones who serve on the behalf of others.

No matter how good a church's plans and programs might be, if there is no person or persons willing, ready and able to execute the program and exercise the plans, things will not be accomplished according to plan.

In the book of **Judges** we find that after Joshua, Moses successor, had brought the Israelites into the land of Palestine and had died, there was a need for a new type of "human instrument" to lead God's people. There arose "judges," whom God appointed and through whom God worked to "administer" the lives of His chosen People.

In the Early Church the Apostle Paul tells us that God Himself has placed in the Church those who have the gift and responsibility of government (**I Corinthians 12:28**). In the New American Standard Bible the work being done is called "administration". In the Revised Standard Version the individuals who do the work are called "administrators." It is clear in Paul's writing that everyone cannot be an apostle, or prophet, or teacher, or miracle worker, or healer, or helper, or administrator, or speak in tongues, or interpret tongues. However, all of these gifts (tasks) are necessary in the life and daily work of the church.

The Apostle Paul speaks in **II Corinthians 8:19-20** of his responsibility of "administration." Some Bible translations change the word "administer" to the word "help." This is unfortunate because the concept of administration is much broader. There are several steps in the administrative process. Each of these steps are necessary and very important.

There is the need of planning where a systematic process is set forth for the accomplishment of the assigned task. Then the administrator must organize and train the staff who are responsible for the work to be done. There is a need for stimulating and motivating the workers, or the task will not be done. Finally there must be ongoing assessment and final evaluation and revision as needed. All of these steps and others the administrator must be able to perform, if things are to be done and done well.

APOSTLE: These are the original witnesses chosen by Christ to "go forth" and carry the Gospel. They were the missionaries of the Early Church. An apostle is one who leads or advocates for a new cause. One who is sent forth; one who goes out as a messenger, and is authorized in a certain way by the one who sends him/her forth. The "apostle" is "he that is sent."

I Corinthians 12:28 states that the first order of persons set in the Church by God is that of "apostle." Also **Ephesians 4:11** tells us that the risen, ascended Christ gave gifts to the Church, and the first of these gifts was that of "apostles."

Observing this order in these two books, it is obvious that the work of the apostle is first and foremost in the fulfilling of the work and the will of God. According to the Book of Ephesians, the "saints," or church members cannot be equipped for ministry (service) without the work of the "apostle." This is not an optional function but rather a necessary and imperative aspect of the Church, which is the Body of Christ.

This being true, the Church must be in prayer, as well as remaining alert, regarding to when, where and to whom this gift will be given. The apostle not only assists in the "perfecting" of the saints for the work of ministry, but also helps to provide for the building up of the Church in the unity of faith, and the knowledge of Christ.

The Christian Church is called to be not only "holy," but also the church is called to be "apostolic." In keeping with this "call," there needs to be a person who embodies this special gift. Paul states in **Romans 1:1** that he was "called to be an apostle," and throughout his writings he refers to himself as an "apostle." The word "apostle" is a New Testament word for a New Testament Church. These are those who are the fulfillment of the Old Testament promise of the Messiah, whose work of salvation would be proclaimed by those who had the task of apostleship.

The first century church grew and spread because of the work of the "apostles." The early adherents to the Christian Faith were those who listened to, and followed, the instructions of the Apostles (**Acts 2:42**). A missing ingredient in the mix of the Christian congregation today may be those who are called and function as apostles. Our task is to pray to the Risen Christ to sent us persons who can be His Apostles, and also to give us the gift of discernment to be able to recognize those persons and the willing spirit to accept and follow those whom Christ gives.

It is this writer's contention that the office and function of "apostles" is no less important in the twentieth or twenty-first century than this gifted person was in the first century. For the church to be all that it can be in this present age, we must have all of the ministries which will make this a reality.

BISHOP: Those who serve as overseers in the Christian Church are called "Bishops". They have the responsibility for providing the oversight for a local church or for a group of churches in a given area. These persons special functions may vary according to the particular need or needs of the church(s). In some situations the responsibility would be more for temporal needs; in some situations the task might be more spiritual; and in still others, the need might be for a combination of both.

A bishop has the responsibility for superintending the total affairs of the church; which includes preparing candidates for membership in the church, teaching the congregation the doctrines of the Faith, and for general care of the members in all matters of church life.

The Apostle Paul spells out in **I Timothy 3:1ff.** and **Titus 1:7ff.** the qualifications of a Bishop. Due to the job expectations, the qualifications for fulfilling the position must be exceptional. It appears from Scripture reading that the office of a Bishop is decided upon by a call from God, an appointment by the Church, and a desire of the individual with the qualifications to fill the office.

COUNSELOR: The task of the counselor is to give advice, direction, or guidance to others. To give advice, one must be knowledgeable of the total situation. This means that they must know the person to whom they are giving advice, and they must have some well informed understanding of the presenting issue or problem. To give biblical counsel, one must have a deep understanding of God's word and a clear understanding when trying to apply God's word to human situations. This calls for the ability to do theological reflection as well as being prayerfully in tune to God's will and God's way.

Not only must the counselor be able to give advice but the counselor must also be able to give direction. It is important not only to tell a person "what" to do but also how to "start," how to "proceed" and how to reach the "goal" or the desired "end." To serve a ministry of "Counsel" is not just to tell a person what to do, but one must be willing to walk with the person through the journey. To be a counselor is to make a commitment to the counselee; to take the same risks; to walk the same path; and to, if necessary, take your own advice.

To be a counselor is to be one who has a deliberate plan, resolution or scheme to address a situation. One who is able to give "informed" opinions in specific situations: An advisor, an attorney, an advocate. To be a counselor is finally one who is willing to not just give guidance and give direction, but one who becomes a guide to lead the counselee by showing as well as telling. A true counselor is one who goes before the other to shine light along the path to the goal. Christ became our High Priest because He was in all ways tempted as we, yet without sin **(Hebrews 4:15)**.

CLERGYPERSON: Those who have been set apart within a local congregation to lead in religious activities, or who renders religious services in church, community or institution. The clergyperson is one who is ordained by God and the local congregation to be the Worship Leader for God's Flock. This might be considered as one function of the Pastor/Shepherd, but this is such an important aspect that in larger Christian communities, this might be a separate and special function. One of the most important duties of God's people is to worship the Lord and give praises to His Holy Name. This cannot happen in our private lives until we have been taught and trained in the matter of public worship.

The clergyperson is "an office worker," and the place of work or service is in the Holy office of the Church. Much of the churches' lack today is in having one who holds this office as being sacred and set apart. To truly lead a congregation means taking the time to know God, His word, His will, and His people. The clergyperson is one who keeps records, correspondence, and who does filing. This means that this person must know intimately the needs and concerns of the worshiper and where that person is in their spiritual journey. Often the leader is leading by "the still waters" when the sheep are still lying "down in green pastures." In order to be a worship leader, one must know who they are leading, where they are, and where they are going.

Then the clergyperson must be "A salesperson for God." There are times when the "sheep" prefer to stay where they are and not be led out into an encounter with God. The Clergyperson must be one who has a meaningful fellowship with God and the enthusiasm to motivate others to share in the fellowship. This means "selling" the worshipers on their need to worship and God's desire to receive their praise.

Finally, the clergyperson must not only be spirit-filled and have a heart on fire for the Lord, but this person must also have knowledge of the office of the clergy. A clergy person must be a literate person and a scholar of God's word.

DEACON: One who assists the clergy in the performance of duties. The task of the clergyperson is so broad that it becomes impossible for one person to fulfill the ministry. One person who is called to assist is the deacon. Most churches have a committee (often called a Board) of deacons. This is understandable because every aspect of church life and service requires someone to assist in the fulfilling of the task. The deacon should assist in the leading of worship, but the deacon should not be the person with primary responsibility.

The deacon is one who works to meet the needs of the people. Both the needs of the leader and the needs of the follower. This is a person who can follow the lead of others and become a helper to all. In worship this person is one who helps the congregation to pray and sing. In other areas of congregational life the deacon is an assistant in the church and a servant to God and His people.

This is a very special ministry because it calls for one to be humble enough to "play second fiddle" and not to seek to be out front or to gain any praise or prestige. Today the Deacon has become a special office and position in the church. In some congregations the deacon is elevated (or elevates himself or herself) above the office of the pastor. Often the position and responsibilities are not spelled out or understood from the beginning. At other times we fail to understand that this function also should be considered as one with a special call by God.

In the early church the deacon, or servant in the church, was chosen through prayer when there was a special need for special assistance. Often the task was time-limited and upon completion of the task the deacon would return to some other place in the life of the congregation.

When the church is determining those it wishes to make workers and ministers within the congregation, it should first determine the needs and ministries needed. Then through prayer and careful consideration the members should choose the best person for the task. This should be a person who is of honest report, and full of the Holy Ghost and wisdom (**Acts 6:3**). A deacon must be "big" enough to fill the job and no "bigger."

DIVINE: A special, holy person who has unique gifts of leadership. This name is seldom used in Scripture to refer to a human, and yet in **II Peter 1:3-4** tells us that *"According as His divine power hath given unto us all things that pertain unto life and godliness, through the knowledge of Him that hath called us to glory and virtue: Whereby are given unto us exceeding great and precious promises: that by these ye* *might be partakers of the DIVINE NATURE, having escaped the corruption that is in the world through lust."*

A divine being is one who is supremely good and who is set off by others in a godlike state and status. In the King James Version, the last book of the New Testament is called "The Revelation of Saint John the Divine." This is the way the early church viewed John the Apostle (probably beginning around the fourth century). There are those who are worshipped by their followers and who are seen as holy individuals who are considered as being "divine."

The church should recognize those who live special saintly lives as a special gift from God to the church and to the given age. There are those whose state of being should give them special status. In sports we elevate athletes and make them "special" role models because they excel in their athletic game and earn very large salaries. Why is it that we do not elevate individuals who exemplify saintly, divine lives and set them up as role models for those who strive to live Godly lives?

The church must discover a means of identifying those who seek to follow the biblical mandate and fulfill the picture of **Psalms 1st Chapter**, and set them apart as those who are truly divine. Saint Paul could say to the Christians of Corinth **(I Corinthians 11:1)** that they should *"Be ye followers (imitators) of me, even as I am of Christ."* These are the kind of "role models" we need today. We are all basically imitators, and Christianity is not only taught but it is also "caught." There is a contagion regarding our Faith and the more a person is filled with the "Fire" of the Holy Spirit, or take on the divine nature, the easier they can ignite the life and fervor of another.

ELDER: Those who have special teaching or pastoral functions in a church. Usually this is a senior or older person; one who is spiritually more mature; or one who has been in the service of God for some time. One who is influential in church and community. The Elder was a male member of the Church who was responsible for the administration of the congregation.

An Elder is one who is older both by nature as well as by maturity. In **I Timothy 3:6** the Apostle Paul states that no one is to be admitted to the office of Elder or Bishop who is a recent convert or novice.

According to **Isaiah 3:2,3** it is the punishment of God when the elder, among other leaders will be taken away and leadership will be performed by children and babes.

Elders were selected on the basis of their age, wisdom, ability, respect and prowess. This person was the head of the home, of the clan or of the community. They were those who would judge in disputes and provide justice for the people. They would sit at the gate and address community situations. The Elders were representatives of the people and defenders of their interests, but without administrative titles. The Elder was more of a function than a title or position.

In **I Peter 5:1**, the Apostle Peter refers to himself as an "elder" when he charges the Elders to *"feed the flock of God."* In **Acts 11:30** there was a collection taken at Antioch for the Elders, and in **Acts 14:23** the Apostle Paul is said to have appointed Elders in every church. In some instances in the New Testament the term "Elder" is used to refer to those chronologically old. At other times it refers to the office of the Elder. In some Christian communities the Elder is seen as being ranked second behind the Priest.

In our youth oriented society, we have lost the place and significance of the "Elder." In the Old Testament **(Exodus 24:1** and **Numbers 11:16)** there was a Council of Seventy Elders, and in the First Century A.D., the Council of Elders was responsible for the government of the Jewish community. The Sanhedrin was a council comprised of seventy-one elders. In the Book of the Revelation, there is the looking forward to the twenty-four elders. In this age of the modern church we have lost the understanding of the place and purpose of the elder in church, clan and community.

EVANGELIST: One who carries and preaches the gospel in a missionary way. One who preaches zealously for the purpose of winning others to the Faith. One whose main purpose for preaching is for soul-winning, to convert others to Christianity and to Christ.

FRIAR: A member of a Roman Catholic order, usually a person who is poor, or, becomes poor, and lives by begging.

FATHER: A father is one who provides structure, discipline and authority in a family. The one who represents authority. To father is to acknowledge something as one's work or creation. In the home, the church, and in the community, fathers have an important role to play. They serve as mentors and models for their sons and they serve as a pattern for their daughters to evaluate other men.

Also there is a need for a father's love and affection in home, church and community. Not only is there a need for the feminine affection, but there is also a need for the masculine attention and affection. We all need the tough mind and the tender heart of the father and the mother to round out our own ability to show and receive love.

Then there is the need for someone to set limits and to be a disciplinarian. This entails the teaching function of the father. As leader of the clan, the father is looked to for instruction and direction. When the father abdicates this role and function, there is anarchy and chaos. The father must be a firm but gentle teacher and guide for the family, both in the home and in the church.

GATEKEEPER: The gatekeeper, doorkeeper, or porter, is one of the key functions and most misunderstood and neglected ministries in the church. David knew and understood the importance of the gatekeeper when he said, *"I had rather be a doorkeeper in the house of my God than dwell in the tents of wickedness"* **(Psalm 84:10)**.

Porters or gatekeepers were used to guard the entrance of public buildings, including the entrance to the temple. They also kept watch over the gates of the cities. Jesus referred to the need for a gatekeeper at the door to a sheepfold (church).

The gatekeeper must be one who knows how to be on watch and who is capable of dealing with any emergency that might arise. The person who has the function of keeping watch over those who come in and go out of God's house must have a discerning spirit. This person must not only be hospitable, but they must also be able to handle dangerous situations where there may be those who seek to enter to do harm to those in the "sheepfold."

HEALER: In **I Corinthians 12:28**, the Apostle Paul lists healing as one of the eight gifts that God has given to the Church. This gift of healing follows the gift of miracles, and throughout the New Testament healing is seen as an integral part of the Church life and work. This is one of the many diverse ministries which was operating in the First Century Church, and is still operating in the Church today. Healing may take many forms and serve many functions. There is a need for personal healing which may relate to the healing of body, soul and/or spirit. There is also the interpersonal need for healing which might include healing of relationships between individuals, groups and ultimately between the individual and God.

There is the need for persons in the congregation to minister to broken persons and to bring wholeness to persons and relationships. This is a demanding task. Scripture tells us that when Jesus effected healing, (virtue) power went out of Him **(Mark 5:30)**. When we allow ourselves to be touched by the problems and pains of hurting souls, we too will experience the depletion of our own power. When we take on others hurt, we make ourselves vulnerable to the same or similar hurt.

The ministry and task of the healer can only be effective when it come as a gift from God. There are many today who seek to heal others with the use of human techniques and therapies. The best that can come of these efforts is that of masking the deep problems and addressing the symptoms of the "disease." Peace and wholeness only come through one who can stand in the "gap" and serve as a reconciler and mediator between the individual and God. Healing is a gift both to the healer and also to the person or persons who are healed. It does not come about because of training, degrees, licenses or certification, but it comes as a Divine gift.

When we reach out and touch a hurting soul, we do not know when, where, how, or if the person will receive healing. This reaching out is an act of faith by the healer that God will bring about healing, and it is a realization by the person with the ministry of healing that God has gifted them as one within the body of Christ who has been called to this special ministry.

HELPER: The ministry of helps is another neglected function in the body of Christ. The Apostle Paul says in **I Corinthians 12:28** that *"God hath set some in the church, first apostles, secondarily prophets, thirdly teachers, after that miracles, then gifts of healing, helps..."* When the ministry of helps is operating within a congregation, every facet of the church life and work is enhanced. If an individual can accomplish a task alone, then the task can be accomplished faster, better and easier when there are others who join in the work. Moses says in **Deuteronomy 32:30** that *"One should chase a thousand, and two put ten thousand to flight..."* When we work together and we develop the ministry of helps, ability is not simply added but multiplied.

Paul says that *"We that are strong ought to bear the infirmities of the weak, and not to please ourselves"* **(Romans 15:1)**. He also calls us to *"Bear one another's burdens, and so fulfil the law of Christ"* **(Galatians 6:2)**.

Both Moses in the Old Testament and Jesus in the New Testament understood and developed this ministry of helps. God gave Moses seventy men to assist him in meeting the children of Israel's needs **(Numbers 11:10-17)**. In **Mark 3:14** Jesus chose twelve disciples to be with Him, and later He appointed seventy others and sent them on ahead of Him, two by two, into every city and place where He himself was about to come **(Luke 10:1)**.

Our ministry falters and fails when we lack those around us who help to share the task and hold up our arms. Every member of the church is placed there by God for a purpose. Each person in the body of Christ has a job to do. Although they may not have a primary task, they can and must share the task of those who are called to be in leadership. The most crucial role is often to be willing, ready and able to play the "second fiddle." These persons also are chosen and anointed by God to serve in His earthly kingdom.

HERALD: This is one who brings news to others. Often the Herald is one who brings "good news," but generally the herald is one who brings a word or message in general. This person is usually not a prophet who either speaks for or as God, but rather one who, as a mail carrier, delivers a message. John saw himself as a herald. He stated that he was only a "voice" crying in the wilderness **(Matthew 3:3)**, while

Jesus stated that John was more that a voice, but also a prophet.

There is the need today, as in the days of the early Church, for men and women to "deliver the mail" and carry the message to the those who need to hear. The herald is not a person who seeks to exhort or interpret but to simply tell the message. An angel is a type of heavenly herald who is used by God to carry a message. There are also those amongst us whose gift and task is to communicate to us what God would have us know. A key distinction between a herald and a prophet or preacher is that the herald remained separate from that which he/she heralded, while often with the prophet and the preacher, the messenger becomes a part of the message.

In Old Testament times the herald is seen as one who runs before the royal chariot to attract the attention of the people, and the herald is responsible for making known the will of the king. Isaiah says that after the herald has cried out for the people to prepare the way of the Lord, then the glory of the Lord will be revealed **(Isaiah 40:5)**.

INTERPRETER: In every community there are not only those who speak, but there are also those who interpret what is said for the benefit of those who are not able to grasp the understanding of what is being said. These persons are called "interpreters" or "discerners." The task of the interpreter varies according to the need of the message being conveyed. There are times when the need is to translate information from one language to another. Then there is the need for an interpreter to explain the meaning of what is said or experienced. Sometimes this is something that is said. At other times this might be something that is experienced in a dream.

Then an interpreter may be an ambassador who represents the will or wishes of another. This other may be a person, or it may be one who interprets the word or will of God. Paul warns that if there is one who speaks in tongues in the congregation, there must also be one with the gift or ability of interpretation present also **(I Corinthians 14:5)**. An interpreter is also one who expounds the Scriptures and makes plain God's word to God's people.

LEADER: In every organization and institution there must be those who are out front and who are able to provide direction and guidance. God places individuals in the Church who have the gift of leadership and He both gives them the responsibility of leadership and He also holds them accountable for the leadership they give to the Church. The leader is a person who has a God-given vision for God's people. God's word **(Proverbs 29:18)** states that *"Where there is no vision, the people perish."* Also where there is no leader with a vision the people will wander in the wilderness of confusion and frustration.

In any organization it is imperative to select or choose a person who is willing, ready and able to give good and effective leadership. It is also imperative to allow God to do the choosing and sending, because we are limited in our assessment of those who have the gifts to lead.

MINISTER: This is a gift that is both specific and also general. On the one hand the person called to be a minister is called to the preaching ministry. On the other hand the person called to be a minister is called to be a "servant" of God and to provide a "service" to, for, and with the People of God. Our problem in the past is that we have made the term "minister" synonymous with the terms "preacher" and "pastor." Because of this limitation of our definition, we have limited the work of the church and the workers in the church.

Here I use the word "minister" in the latter sense of one who has been called into the preaching and/or pastoral ministry. This book, however, is an attempt to see the ministry and the minister in the broadest sense possible.

MISSIONARY: This is the person who is sent out to perform a ministry, or a service outside of the Church. This ministry, or task, might be religious or it may be social, political, educational, etc. It means to be one who does a work for God in the world, whether at home or abroad.

NEOPHYTE: This is a minister in training. To be a "neophyte" is to be an apprentice; one who is learning and growing to the fullness of stature both spiritually and functionally. In a sense we are all neophytes, because none of us have risen to the fullness of our stature to be in the likeness of Christ.

There are some persons in the Christian body who have not matured to the place where they can be of more help than harm to others. Even as the doctor must spend many hours in training and then the rest of his/her life in practice the Christian worker must also first be trained then practice. One of the great dangers and draw-backs in many of our churches is that there are many people in ministry who are not equipped for the task to which they have been assigned or equipped to the position which they have chosen. Paul cautions against the quick ordination of a neophyte to the position of overseer or the elevation of a novice to a position of leadership **(I Timothy 3:6)**.

OFFICER: There are those who have a function in the Church body. There are others who have a place or position. The Church is not only an organism, but it is also an organization. In order for the Church to function as an organization there must be structure and there must be some form of hierarchy within the structure. There are those with administrative ability who are called to be "officers" in the Church. **I Corinthians 12:28** tells us that God has set some in the church to be governments, or administrators or managers. When the church has persons in official positions who know how to manage and administer the affairs, and when the church understands the function and need of these officers; and the church is willing to follow these managers and administrators, the church will progress in fulfilling its mission.

PRIEST: While there are congregations and denominations who hold to the teaching of "The priesthood of all believers", there is still a need for a person or persons to be designated to the specific task of the Priest. One thing needed in the Church is to have mentors and role models. There is the need for those in the body of Christ to show us by example how we are to fulfill our calling of being a "royal Priesthood" **(I Peter 2:9)**.

The priest was one who was able to comprehend the will of God; to be holy and consecrated to the will of God; to perform the work of God, and to follow in the way of God. This is what the Apostle Peter tells us. We are to be lively stones which are built up into a spiritual house filled with those who are a "holy priesthood", offering spiritual gifts to God **(I Peter 2:5)**. We can do this best when there are those with the special vocation within the Church which we can imitate, as Paul told the Church of his day to imitate (or follow) him as he followed Christ.

PASTOR: Although this is an overused word and concept in our churches today, and it is the aspiration of many who come into the church and who seek to attain to the "high office" of "Pastor", this is a little used word in the Bible. In the Old Testament the word is used once in the singular form and seven times in the plural form. It basically is used to mean to "tend a flock," or to keep company with."

In the New Testament the word "pastor" is used once as a title in **Ephesians 4:11** where Paul gives the categories of Christian workers. However, the function of "pastor" is found throughout the Old and the New Testament. Our confusion today is that we think that the office of "pastor" is a high office rather than a lowly service. Jesus told His disciples, and He tells us today, that if you desire to be great, you must be a servant **(Mark 10:43)**.

PROPHET: The Church has a prophetic ministry, therefore it must have those with a prophetic calling and a prophetic ministry. This is a "heavenly" calling and must not be entered into lightly. Today there are many who call themselves "prophet." Many of those who call themselves or are called by others, have not been called by God. The danger of false prophets is that they lead people falsely. The question is whether the prophets are false or whether the people who follow them are false. If people start out with the wrong leaders, and are going in the wrong direction, it is certain that they will end up at the wrong destination.

A Prophet is not only one who fore-tells but also forth-tells. Today we have many who are seeking to tell us our future, and there are many who spend a lot of money, time and effort to seek out these psychic individuals and follow their suggestions for their future. The scriptures warn us over and over again about the danger of looking for "signs" and following soothsayers. And yet we refuse to listen to the word of

God but will listen to the cunning words of people.

God has placed in the Church prophets (**I Corinthian 12:28; Ephesians 4:11**) to speak forth His word. Notice in both of these scriptures that the prophet is second in the list of those placed in the Church by God. First in both lists is the ministry of the Apostle. Also in the First Church the people first listened steadfastly to the teachings of the apostles (**Acts 2:42**). Because of their understanding of the place and function of ministers in the early church, the number grew and multiplied.

TEACHER: When Paul gives the qualifications of the bishop or overseer or head of the local church, he says that the bishop must be "apt to teach" (**I Timothy 23:2**). Again Paul tells Timothy (**II Timothy 2:25**) to "**Study to shew thyself approved unto God, a workman that needeth not to be ashamed, rightly dividing the word of truth.**"

Before one can be a leader they must first be a follower, and before one can be a teacher, they must first be a student. We cannot lead where we will not go and we cannot teach what we do not know. This knowledge must be deeper that intellectual knowledge, but it must also be a spiritual knowledge through a personal and intimate experience with Jesus Christ.

The above list and explanations do not begin to exhaust the areas and diversities of ministries needed in today's Church in order to adequately minister to today's world. This is only intended to get the reader to thinking how vast the mission of the Church is and how varied the ministry of the Church must become so that we as the Church, the Body of our Lord Jesus Christ, can fulfill the desire of Paul to truly become all things to all people (**I Corinthians 9:22**).

CHAPTER 10

THE DESTINATION OF THE MINISTRY

Every ministry not only has a beginning but also to be truly a God-given ministry, it must also have an end. Jesus told His disciples to begin their ministry at Jerusalem, but to continue it to the end of the earth **(Matthew 28:16-20; Acts 1:8)**. God never does a job half-way. In **Deuteronomy 6:23**, Moses says *"And He (God) brought us out from thence, that He might bring us in, to give us the land which he swore by our fathers."* God always has a plan and a purpose in mind when He performs a work in us or in our midst. Our ministry must also have a purpose if it is a vocation from God.

We must have a sense of both our departure into the ministry, and we must also have a sense of our destination as we move along in our ministry. The only way we shall be able to judge and evaluate our ministry is to have a sense of our goal. Though the Apostle Paul says that *"we know in part..."* and that *"now we see through a glass, darkly,"* yet we must have some sense of destination in order to determine our direction.

The Christian Faith and the Christian Church is not only a historical religion, but it is also a teleological religion. In other words we not only have a beginning as a religious movement, when Christ said, *"upon this rock I will build my church..."*, and when the church was launched into the future with Power on the day of Pentecost **(Acts 2:1ff**; the Christian Church has an end when Christ shall come for His Church **(I Thessalonians 4:14-18; Titus 2:13,** etc.).

The gospel of **Matthew 24:24** tells us of the destination of our mission and our ministry. There it is written, *"And this gospel of the kingdom shall be preached in all the world for a witness unto all nations; and then shall the end come."* Our mission and our ministry has been pre-determined by the Head of the Church, our Lord Jesus Christ. He is Alpha and Omega, the First and Last, the Beginning and the END; the Author and Finisher of our faith **(Revelation 1:11, 21:6, 22:13; Hebrews 12:2)**.

To understand the concept of goal setting, and the practical application and determination of our destination, is key to the work of the church and its many ministries. When we set goals we are better able to plan, organize and measure our work and our progress. When we have a sense of what we are doing and where we are going, we can do better work with less time and effort. Not only will we be able to determine where we are going and how we are getting there, but others will also have a sense of out mission and our ministry.

Many churches are drifting aimlessly today or moving in circles because there is no understanding of mission and no sense of the multi-faceted ministry to which the church has been called. Many churches are caught up in work of maintenance while others have a narrow focus on "being religious" or "being a social club," while the true work of the church is being neglected and the true goal of the church is being lost. God's word is a "Road Map" to guide the Church in its mission and lead it to its desired end. **Psalm 119:105** says *"Thy word is a lamp unto my feet, and a light unto my path."* Many churches today are walking in darkness because they have lost the light (the "road map" which is God's Holy Word), or they either fail to read the "map", or they do not know how to *"rightly divide the word of truth"* **(I Timothy 2:15)**. To not know or to not understand are both equally dangerous.

We cannot adequately use our gifts, skills, talents, or abilities; on the one hand, until we have an awareness of what they are, how they fit into God's plan for His Church and His world. On the other hand, we cannot fully utilize these gifts, skills, talents and abilities until we are *"able to comprehend with all saints what is the breadth, and length, and depth, and height;"* **(Ephesians 3:18)**, of our ministry and our mission. Our ministry informs us of "what" we are called to do in our service to God and humanity. This is the scope of our ministry, the depth and breath of our service. This ministry also tells us "who" we are called to serve. We are to minister to all people in every nation. Our mission tells us "when" and "where" we are to perform our mission. This tells us how our mission is to "stretch" to the end of the earth and to the end of the age. This tells us of the length and the height of our mission.

If we fail to comprehend this magnitude of our ministry and our mission, then we have failed to grasp the "Great Commission" of our Lord Jesus Christ, and, therefore, we fail to be His Church and we have become "our little churches." If this becomes a fact, then even our best efforts will fail, and even though Christ says that the gates of hell will not prevail against His Church, our little societies will become the very "gates of hell." We will increase in numbers of members and our budget will increase, but we will only be like those whom Jesus chastised in **Matthew 23rd chapter** who compass sea and land to make one proselyte, and when he is made, *"ye make him twofold more the child of hell than yourselves"*. Because we fail to understand the scope of Christian mission and ministry, and God's Word is not Light to guide us, we are like "blind leaders of the blind."

In order for the minister to meet his/her desired end, there are three things which must be given initial and continuous consideration. The first consideration has to do with the outlook of the task to be accomplished. What is the intention or the purpose for which this ministry has begun or this ministry is being attempted? How does our plan fit in with God's will and plan for the Christian minister or the church ministry? Is our aim and desire for service in the body of Christ based on a divine call and commission or are we seeking to do our own will?

The second thing which must be considered as we seek to fulfill our mission and ministry is to be certain of our orientation. Are we focused in the right direction and are our means ethical and biblical or are we moving in the wrong direction. There are those who believe that we may achieve our ends "by any means necessary," and there are those who believe that all roads will lead us to the desired end. Jesus says in His Sermon on the Mount that we must choose the "strait gate", because *"broad is the way, that leadeth to destruction, and many there be which go in thereat: Because strait is the gate, and narrow is the way, which leadeth unto life, and few there be that find it."* **(Matthew 7:13-14)**. If it is our desire that our ministry and our church's mission have value and true life, we must be sure that we are focused in the right direction.

Jesus told His First Century disciples and He tells those of us in the Twentieth Century (and moving into the Twenty-first Century) that is we desire to be successful in our ministry we must *"Cast the net on the right side of the ship, and ye shall find"* **(John 21:6)**. Because we fail to follow our Master's direction and seek to win souls by our means and methods, many would-be Christians are lost. Isaiah **(Isaiah 5:13-14)** says that *"Therefore My people are gone into captivity, because they have no knowledge... Therefore hell hath enlarged herself, and opened her mouth without measure."* If we do not follow God's program for ministry, we become enemies of His plan for salvation and our efforts enhance the kingdom of Satan.

The third thing that we must consider, as we seek to fulfill our task, is the desired outcome which we hope to achieve. This has to do with not only our deployment and direction, but it has to do with our destination. This has to do with our short-term objective for a particular task and not our final goal for the end of the age. Working in the church's ministry is similar to eating an elephant. We must achieve our final goal "one bite at a time." We must break up the overall task of the church into small achievable tasks where we can evaluate our progress and move on ahead to other objectives as needed.

As we consider the outlook, the orientation, and the outcome of our task, we must do this in seven significant areas. Each of these areas must work together to achieve the total mission of the Church. If we fail in any one of these areas we cause the work of the Church to develop abnormally and lose its God-determined destiny. "Seven" in the Scripture is a number which signifies spiritual perfection, a number of completion. When the church's ministry encompasses the following aspects, then its mission is being completed, its life is being perfected, and the church is worshipping God in spirit and in truth. The seven areas and aspects of mission and ministry are as follows:

1. THAT SINNERS WILL BE JUSTIFIED:

While God's word tells us in **Romans 8:33** that *"It is God that justifieth,"* the Christian and the Christian Church have a mission and a ministry in the work of justification in the sinner's life. It is the work of the saint to bring the sinner into a saving relation with God so that the sinner's life can be changed and made righteous before God. As Andrew brought his brother, Peter, to the Lord, and as Philip brought

Nathanael to the Lord, **(John 1:41, 45)** so too we must seek to bring the lost to the Lord.

The preaching of the Gospel and the witnessing of the Church to the love of God causes the sinner to seek to experience the acceptance of God. The Church reaching out to the sinner in a vast array of ministries is like the fisherman casting the net into the deep. Every ministry in the church that plays a part in this ministry allows the Church of Jesus Christ to fulfill its purpose. Jesus stated that he came *"to seek and save that which is lost."* That which is lost is the sinner who has not found the Savior, or the sinner that has not been found by the Savior. Christ uses us as His hands and feet to bring lost souls to a saving relation with Him. This is the work of the church until the end of the age.

2. **THAT THE WORK OF GOD WILL BE MULTIPLIED:**

Our goal is to proclaim the gospel to every creature, in every nation, until the end of time. Our first responsibility as a people of God is evangelistic. As a church we are to seek to be creative in finding ways to share the good news. We are not only to apply various means but we are also to employ various men and women in the work of communicating the gospel.

We are called to be co-laborers with Christ and to be mutually supportive of each other. The work is too great for any one denomination to attempt, and the work of the local church is too large for the pastor and a few faithful members to attempt alone. There must be a team effort and there must be a diversity of people, programs and participation.

Paul says in **I Corinthians 12:4-11**, *"Now there are diversities of gifts, but the same Spirit. And there are differences of administrations, but the same Lord. And there are diversities of operations, but it is the same God which worketh all in all. But the manifestation of the Spirit is given to every man to profit withal. For to one is given by the Spirit the word of wisdom; to another the word of knowledge by the same Spirit; to another faith by the same Spirit; to another the gifts of healing by the same Spirit; to another the working of miracles; to* *another discerning of spirits; to another divers kinds of tongues: But all these worketh that one and the selfsame Spirit, dividing to every man severally as he will."*

3. **THAT THE WORD OF GOD WILL BE MAGNIFIED:**

Our aim and purpose as Christians and as the Christian Church is to continue to tell the story of our Faith. The Great Command in the gospels is that we go every where and tell all people for all ages the Good News of God's great plan of salvation.

The Apostle speaks of the importance of the spoken word. In **Romans 10:14, 17-18,** he says, *"How shall they call on Him in whom they have not believed? and how shall they believe in Him of whom they have not heard? and how shall they hear without a preacher? So faith cometh by hearing, and hearing by the word of God. But I say, Have they not heard? Yes verily, their sound went into all the earth, and their words unto the ends of the world."*

David says in **Psalm 19:1-4** that *"The heavens declare the glory of God; and the firmament sheweth His handiwork. Day unto day uttereth speech, and night unto night sheweth knowledge. There is no speech nor language where His voice is not heard."* Jesus told the Pharisees who complained about the people speaking of Him in Old Testament prophesy, that *"If these should hold their peace, the stones would immediately cry out"* **(Luke 19:40)**. All of nature proclaims the mighty works of God, and it is the mission and ministry of the Church to join in with the proclamation of the Word. As stated above, "This gospel of the Kingdom shall be preached in all the world for a witness unto all nations; and then shall the end come" **(Matthew 24:14)**. **Matthew 28:19-20** gives us Christ's command to His Church to, *"Go ye therefore, and teach all nations, baptizing them in the name of the Father, and of the Son, and of the Holy Ghost: Teaching them to observe all things whatsoever I have commanded you: and, lo, I am with you alway, even unto the end of the world. Amen."* **Mark 16:20** concludes that Gospel by stating the Disciples' compliance to Christ's command. *"And they went forth, and preached everywhere, the Lord working with them, and* confirming the word with signs following." The

Acts of The Apostles is the story of how the preaching, teaching, and witnessing of the "mighty acts of God" spread from Jerusalem, throughout all of Judea, into Samaria, and unto the ends of the earth.

Also the History of the Church down through the ages to the present time is a History of how the People of God continue to spread the Gospel story to every generation, to every nation, and to every tongue. The story of Pentecost is a story which tells us of our ability, aided by the Holy Spirit, to proclaim repentance and remission of sins among all nations.

4. THAT THE CHURCH WILL BE EDIFIED:

In order for the Church to be the Church, and in order for the Church to grow and develop in the way that God has intended, there is a need for continued edification of those who are a part of the Church. To "edify" is to teach, instruct, or enlighten so as to encourage moral, intellectual, or spiritual improvement. **Ephesians 4:10-16** states that when Christ ascended "up far above the heavens", He gave gifts unto men. *"And He gave some, apostles; and some prophets; and some evangelists; and some, pastors and teachers; for the perfecting of the saints, for the work of the ministry, for the edifying of the body of Christ...From whom the whole body fitly joined together and compacted by that which every joint supplieth, according to the effectual working in the measure of every part, maketh increase of the body unto the edification of itself in love."*

In **I Corinthians 14:4b**, Paul says *"Let all things be done unto edifying."* The goal, and aim of the work within the local church is to build up the individual and the congregation so that ALL of its members might be equipped to fulfill its mission and to be fully engaged in its many ministries.

Hebrews 5:12 speaks of the writers concern regarding the state of the Church. He says, *"For when for the time ye ought to be teachers, ye have need that one teach you again which be the first principles of the oracles (i.e., words, revelation, counsel, commands) of God; and are become such as have need of milk, and not of strong meat."*

The Church in many areas has become ineffective today because of the lack of edifying being done in the Church. Many churches are caught up in "signs and wonders" which does not equip the saints for ministry nor does it edify the saints. Paul warns the Christians at Corinth **(I Corinthians 14:3-4)** *"But he that prophesieth speaketh unto men to edification, and exhortation, and comfort. He that speaketh in an unknown tongue edifieth himself; but he that prophesieth edifieth the Church."*

When Paul speaks of "prophesying" he means not so much that a person would "foretell" the future, but rather that the person would "forth-tell" or to tell forth the decrees of God and the doctrine of the Church. The task of prophesying in this instance is the work of the preacher and teacher.

The destination of the ministry within the Church is, therefore that each member will *"come in the unity of the faith, and of the knowledge of the Son of God, unto a perfect man, unto the measure of the stature of the fullness of Christ: That we henceforth be no more children, tossed to and fro, and carried about with every wind of doctrine, by the sleight of men, and cunning craftiness, whereby they lie in wait to deceive; but speaking the truth in love, may grow up into Him in all things..."* **(Ephesians 4:14-15)**. This is the vocation to which we have been called; that we become enlightened intellectually, morally, and spiritually to the glory of God.

5. **THAT THE SOCIETY WILL BE PURIFIED:**

In Christ's first sermon as recorded by Matthew (The Sermon on the Mount), Jesus told His disciples that they (and we) are the "salt" of the earth and the "light" of the world. If there is conflict, corruption, decay, and destruction in our society today, we must look at the Church not as the cause but as the remedy for our societal condition. The destination of the work of the Church is to bring about a better world, or rather to bring about a world that conforms to the will and the word of God.

Jesus' first sermon according to Luke was preached in His hometown. He quoted from the Old Testament prophet, **(Isaiah 61:1-3)** *"The Spirit of the Lord God is upon me; because the Lord hath* *anointed me to preach good tidings unto the meek; He hath sent me to bind up the broken-hearted, to proclaim liberty to the captives, and the opening of the prison to them that are bound; To proclaim the acceptable year of the Lord."*

When Jesus was asked by the disciples of John the Baptist if He was *"He that should come"* or should they look for another; *"Then Jesus answering them said unto them, Go your way, and tell John what things ye have seen and heard; how that the blind see, the lame walk, the lepers are cleansed, the deaf hear, the dead are raised, to the poor the gospel is preached."* **(Luke 7:19-22)**. Jesus' mission and ministry was measured by its fruits. So too should the Church of Christ be able to point to the effects that it has on its time and its environment.

The Church is in the world to make the world better. Often the world changes the Church more than the Church is able to change the world. In Jesus' Sermon on the Mount, He warns His followers of the danger of the "salt" losing it savour or of the "light" being hidden under a bushel. We must let our light shine and we must purify a world that will perish without a vision of a mission and a ministry that will reach out and touch all people everywhere.

Even as the Church is being edified, it must also move out into the world to share what it has and to win others to the body of Christ. We cannot wait until we have achieved completeness before we reach out to others. We must go forth in faith believing that God, through His Holy Spirit will enable us to perform our ministry and complete our mission. Paul says even from a prison cell, *"But my God shall supply all your need according to His riches in glory by Christ Jesus"* **(Philippians 4:19)**. Because it is God's will that none be lost, our task has His endorsement and we have His constant benediction. The prayer of our Lord Jesus Christ was that our Father's Kingdom will come on earth as it is in Heaven. All that we have to do is go out into the "highways and hedges" and unto the ends of the earth and proclaim the good news. God's word will not return unto Him void.

6. **THAT GOD WILL BE GLORIFIED:**

At the end of Christ's earthly ministry He prayed *"Father, glorify*

Thy name. Then came there a voice from heaven, saying, I have both glorified it, and will glorify it again" **(John 12:28)**. In the life, death, resurrection and ascension of Jesus Christ, God's name received glory. Also when the people of God fulfill the will and word of God, His name is glorified again. The end of man is to bring glory unto God. We are called to live in such a way that we will be able to *"prove what is that good, and acceptable, and perfect, will of God"* **(Romans 12:2b)**.

When we speak of the "glory" of God we mean both His inherent, or essential character, and also we speak of the adoration, praise, honor, which we ascribe to Him. God is ALL glorious, but it is the mission of the Church and its destination and end, to so magnify the God of Grace and Glory that all creatures will realize His greatness. **Isaiah 40:4-5** says that when *"Every valley shall be exalted, and every mountain and hill shall be brought low: and the crooked shall be made straight, and the rough places plain: "then," The glory of the Lord shall be revealed, and all flesh shall see it together: for the mouth of the Lord hath spoken it".*

This whole fact of God's glory is both realized in the present and expected in the future. **II Corinthians 4:6** tells us that it is in the face of Christ that the light of the knowledge of the glory of God shines in our hearts with creative power. Throughout the New Testament Christ is presented as the glory of God made visible on earth to those whose eyes are opened to see it. In John's Gospel we see more clearly throughout his writings this concept or reality of the glory of Christ, the Son of God, and the glory of God, the Father of Christ. **John 1:14** says *"We beheld His glory, the glory as of the only begotten of the Father, full of grace and truth."*

The Apostle Paul speaks not only of the glory of Christ but also of the glory which belongs to the Body of Christ, the Church. In his prayer for the Church at Ephesus Paul concludes by praying *"Now unto Him that is able to do exceeding abundantly above all that we ask or think, according to the power that worketh in us, Unto Him be glory in the church by Christ Jesus throughout all ages, world without end. Amen"* **(Ephesians 3:20-21)**. Because God has chosen to work through the Church in this dispensation of grace, He has also chosen to give His glory to the Church and to its ministry. The glory of Christ and the glory of the Church is not the glory of men, but it is the glory of God. **Romans 8:30** says, *"Moreover whom He (God) did predestinate, them He also called: and whom He called, them He also justified: and whom He justified, them He also glorified."*

The Church is not only a special institution. It is also a sacred organization and organism, because God's presence dwells within the members of the congregation. The glory that we manifest is the reflected Glory of God, through Christ, by the power of His Holy Spirit. We can say like Paul **(Philippians 4:13)**, *"I can do all things through Christ which strengtheneth me."*

7. THAT WRONG WILL BE RECTIFIED:

The work of the Church, its mission and its ministry is to proclaim the TRUTH. Paul told Timothy **(II Timothy 2:15)** to *"Study to shew thyself approved unto God, a workman that needeth not to be ashamed, rightly dividing the word of truth."* In **II Timothy 3:16-17** Paul says *"All scripture is given by inspiration of God, and is profitable for doctrine, for reproof, for correction, for instruction in righteousness: That the man of God may be perfect, thoroughly furnished unto all good works."* God's word is able to make us wise unto salvation and also able to enable us to right the wrongs in Church and society.

David cries out in **Psalm 43:3**, *"O send out Thy light and Thy truth: let them lead me; let them bring me unto Thy holy hill, and to Thy tabernacles."* It is only through God's word and God's truths that we are able to address the ills and wrongs of our time. We are called to confront wrong not with philosophy, the thinking of man, nor teachings from the tree of knowledge of good and evil, but we are to address the subtle and crafty wiles of the evils in our society with the illumination and revelation which is from God.

Jesus said to His disciples in the first century and He says to those of us who are His followers today, *"If ye continue in my word, then are ye my disciples indeed; And ye shall know the truth, and the truth shall set you free"* **(John 8:31b-32).** It is only when we follow the true teachings and when we teach the true precepts of God that we are free from confusion, deception, error and folly. Paul warns young Timothy **(II Timothy 4:3-4)** *"For the time will come when they will not endure sound doctrine; but after their own lusts shall heap to themselves teachers, having itching ears; And they shall turn away their ears from the truth, and shall be turned unto fables."*

We live in an age when wrong is applauded and right is crucified. There is so much confusion through the media, the various religions which seemingly spring up over night, and the convincing rhetoric of those who claim to be a spokesperson for God, that it is becoming increasingly difficult for the masses to know what truth is and to accept the right teachings. God says through the Old Testament prophet, Hosea, **(Hosea 4:6)**, *"My people are destroyed for lack of knowledge."* Today we are not sure which way is up or which way will lead us to peace, prosperity and sanity. The Church must become the "avant garde" to lead the world out of darkness into the Light and to lead the people of God to our final destination, the Kingdom of God. For us to realize our destination we must multiply the ministry of the Church and stretch the scope of sacred service into the secular society.

CONCLUSION

In conclusion, I consider the present task of the Church of Jesus Christ to be that of continuing to stretch the scope of the service of the Church, the sacred community, until it penetrates and permeates every aspect of secular society. The Church of our Lord Jesus Christ is called to be fully the salt of the earth and the light of the world. We must continue to stretch and strive to multiply the ministries within the Church and magnify the mission of the Church until our effects are realized to the ends of the earth and to the end of the age.

We must continue to expand our efforts and expend our energies so that when Christ comes for His Church He will find us not "stained" but "stretched" to our greatest capacity. Then we will hear our Lord say, *"Well done, good and faithful servant; thou hast been faithful over few things, I will make thee ruler over many things: enter thou into the joy of thy Lord"* **(Matthew 25:23)**.

Our final destination is summed up in the words recorded by the Apostle John in **Revelation 7:9-17**; *"I beheld, and, lo, a great multitude, which no man could number, of all nations, and kindreds, and people, and tongues, stood before the Lamb, clothed with white robes, and palms in their hands... These are they which came out of great tribulation, and have washed their robes, and made them white in the blood of the Lamb. Therefore are they before the throne of God, and serve Him day and night in His temple: and He that sitteth on the throne shall dwell among them... and God shall wipe away all tears from their eyes."* Amen.

SCRIPTURE INDEX (Alphabetically arranged)

SUBJECT INDEX

ORDER FORM

To order additional copies of **Stretching The Scope of Sacred Service**, complete the information below.

Ship to: (please print)

Name: ______________________________

Address: ______________________________

City, State, Zip: ______________________________

Day phone: (___) ____________________

_____ copies of *Stretching The Scope* @ $12.95 each $________

Postage and handling @ $2.50 per book $ ________

Massachusetts residents add 5% tax $ ________

Total amount enclosed $ ________

Make checks payable to **Everette W. Frye, Sr.**

Send to: **Frye POWER Publishing Concern**
Post Office Box 750
Lynn, MA 01903-0950

For questions or phone orders call:
1-888-217-5352 or **1-617-595-1516**

ORDER FORM

To order additional copies of **Stretching The Scope of Sacred Service**, complete the information below.

Ship to: (please print)

Name: ______________________________

Address: ______________________________

City, State, Zip: ______________________________

Day phone: (___) ____________________

_____ copies of *Stretching The Scope* @ $12.95 each $________

Postage and handling @ $2.50 per book $ ________

Massachusetts residents add 5% tax $ ________

Total amount enclosed $ ________

Make checks payable to **Everette W. Frye, Sr.**

Send to: **Frye POWER Publishing Concern**
Post Office Box 750
Lynn, MA 01903-0950

For questions or phone orders call:
1-888-217-5352 or **1-617-595-1516**

ORDER FORM

To order additional copies of **Stretching The Scope of Sacred Service**, complete the information below.

Ship to: (please print)

Name: ______________________________

Address: ______________________________

City, State, Zip: ______________________________

Day phone: (___) ______________________

_____ copies of *Stretching The Scope* @ $12.95 each $________

Postage and handling @ $2.50 per book $ ________

Massachusetts residents add 5% tax $ ________

Total amount enclosed $ ________

Make checks payable to **Everette W. Frye, Sr.**

Send to: **Frye POWER Publishing Concern**
Post Office Box 750
Lynn, MA 01903-0950

For questions or phone orders call:
1-888-217-5352 or **1-617-595-1516**